D THIS DAILY

LAN PHAN

THIN LEAF PRESS | LOS ANGELES

D

THIS

DAILY

Secrets to Finding Success, Happiness, and Purpose in Work and Life

Stop Waiting for Someone to Save You, You Have Always Been the Hero in Your Story

Library of Congress Cataloging-in-Publication Data
Names: Phan, Lan
Title: *Do This Daily: Secrets to Finding Success, Happiness & Purpose in Work and Life*
LCCN: 2023922154

ISBN 978-1-953183-36-1 (hardcover) | 978-1-953183-35-4 (paperback)
ISBN 978-1-953183-34-7 (eBook) | 978-1-953183-37-8 (audiobook)
Leadership, Business, Professional Development
Cover Design: 100 Covers
Interior Design: Formatted Books
Illustrations: Van Phan, Morgan Messam & Ekaterina Korol
Editor: Erik Seversen
Thin Leaf Press
Los Angeles

THIN
LEAF

"Fake it till you make it is empty advice. Instead, we become by doing. Becoming requires that we start before we are ready. That's how we become. Don't fake it till you make it. **DO IT DAILY** until you become it."

–Lan Phan

CONTENTS

Hello, Raindrops!

This book bears a heartfelt dedication to you. For the past few years, I've called the community of leaders who read my content Raindrops. Now, you are a part of this community. Welcome!

Why Raindrops you might ask?

We are the empaths and the givers in the world. A Raindrop believes that each of us has a purpose in life, and our mission is to figure out that purpose. We've been taught that our empathy and kindness is a weakness by those who are much louder, but we now understand that when we give each other permission to live authentically, we realize our collective impact knows no end. When we come together, we have the power to change the world for the better.

We are all like Raindrops.

What we do seems small and inconsequential, but when we come together, we become the ocean.

It's this ocean that creates ripples, that turn into waves.

It is these same waves that transform the earth and give it life. Never forget the immense power water has, for it can chisel through rocks, corrode elements, and give life and nourishment. Remember, Raindrops, when we come together, we can transform the earth.

This is how we change the world, one raindrop at a time.

Love,

#DoThisDaily

Lean in closer: I'd like to request a small favor. If you could take a moment to share pictures of yourself holding this book, perhaps with a favorite page or a meaningful quote, or give a testimonial about how this book has impacted you and share on social media. This would mean the world to me. Don't forget to use the hashtag **#DoThisDaily.** I'll do my best to like your post and even feature it on my page.

And if you enjoy this book, it would mean the world if you could review it on Amazon.com, Goodreads.com, or wherever you purchased the book. That's how you give us writers a big bear hug!

Together, let's create a ripple around the world, Raindrops!

Thank you!

"Walk through the universe
as if it's already yours."

–Lan Phan

INTRODUCTION

What matters most to you?

What makes your heart sing?

What is your life's purpose?

If you were like me, you would have difficulty answering those questions. I didn't find answers until a few years ago when a professional setback sent me on a long journey of self-discovery.

In early 2020, I occupied a prominent executive position at Fortune Magazine, reporting to the CEO. As an intrapreneur, I had been entrusted with a multi-million-dollar budget to cultivate a startup under the magazine's esteemed brand. With plans to assemble a team of 100 and launch a product within six months, I was poised for success. However, fate took an unexpected turn. At the onset of the COVID-19 pandemic, I received the devastating news of my layoff just as I was hiring my fifth team member. In addition to my departure, I was tasked with the painful responsibility of dismantling my entire team.

For lack of a better term, the following weeks sucked. I surrendered to depression, cloaked in the same sweatpants and shirt for two weeks. There were moments when I couldn't muster the energy to leave my bed. Though I had encountered bouts of depression and anxiety in the past, this instance felt like an unending abyss with no glimmer of hope.

Worries and fears inundated my thoughts. How would I manage to pay the mortgage? How would I still be able to care for my 85-year-old mother with dementia? How was I going to find a job during a pandemic? How could we afford health insurance? What if my family contracted Covid without health insurance? Why me?

During this dark period, my focus was consumed entirely by my fears and what I wanted to avoid. I wasn't out of my stupor when my five-year-old daughter, Morgan, spoke up. "Mommy, I love you, even without a job," were the words I desperately needed to hear. In that poignant moment, I realized I had been selfishly absorbed in my grief, neglecting the needs of those around me.

It dawned on me that I had become so fixated on my losses that I had grown disconnected from what mattered most: my family. If I could so quickly lose sight of my profound love for my daughter, what other core values had I neglected?

Finding My Purpose

From that point onward, I grappled with a profound question: What mattered most to me? It struck me that, as a grown woman, I had never asked myself this simple yet profound question. I had lived much of my life conforming to other people's expectations and catering to their desires. In my youth, it was my parents; during my teens, it was my peers; and in my twenties, it was my bosses or significant others.

In my quest to unearth my authentic purpose, I embarked on an exhaustive journey of introspection. I began to scrutinize every facet of my existence, reevaluating what truly mattered to me and expressing these sentiments to others. I rekindled relationships with friends and family members I had lost touch with over months and years. Meditation became a source of solace. I placed a heightened focus on my mental and physical well-being. And for the first time in my adult life, I prioritized myself.

As this lengthy journey neared its end, I discovered that what genuinely mattered to me, and had always mattered, were my family, the friends who had become my chosen family, my faith, the act of serving others, and my freedom.

My North Star: Living My Values

Upon recognizing my core values, it became clear that I had not been living a life that honored them, not even my top value, my family. I had been toiling in jobs that saw me leaving home at dawn and returning well past midnight, leaving me with scant moments to spend with my daughter and husband during the workweek. I was often too exhausted to be fully present for them on the weekends. How could I claim that my family was my priority if I scarcely saw them? A glaring contradiction existed between my professed values and how I led my life.

I had failed to live a life guided by my core values, guiding principles, and beliefs, acting as my North Star. If each of us possesses an internal compass, and our core values serve as the cardinal directions on that compass, I came to the stark realization that I could never truly realize my purpose in life if I remained ignorant of what mattered to me. At that pivotal moment, I understood that I had to begin living in alignment with my values in every facet of my life.

A Book Born Out of Community

In my professional journey, I embarked on a path aligned with my core value of serving others. I started small: a pledge to regularly meet with the five team members I had just laid off from Fortune Magazine. My heart ached for them, knowing that some had resigned from their previous positions just a week before joining my team. I assured them that I would meet with them until they all secured new job opportunities or until I had the chance to build a company and could hire them back. I was wholeheartedly committed to their success because they resembled my younger self—women striving to carve their paths in the corporate world. As a woman of color, I intimately understood the extra hurdles underrepresented individuals face in corporate landscapes.

Our collective, dubbed the "Community of Seven," included my five-year-old daughter as our seventh member, who occasionally joined our Zoom calls during the pandemic. Little did I realize then that this weekly ritual would set in motion a series of events that would enable me to serve millions and author this book.

Each month, the team would find their next opportunity, and we cheered each other every time. The success of the Community of Seven served as my inspiration to embark on a venture of establishing a company. I recognized the glaring absence of enough women in leadership roles to encourage and empower fellow women to pursue their aspirations.

Initially, I grappled with a strong sense of impostor syndrome. Who was I to venture into entrepreneurship in my forties, especially during a pandemic when my family depended on me? Doubt cast a long shadow over me, threatening to consume my resolve.

From Knowing to Doing

To conquer my doubts, I embarked on a simple yet transformative journey—I began posting daily on social media. These posts served as daily reminders of the power of perseverance and continual progress. At the outset, I penned these messages primarily for my benefit. I was writing for people like me: the givers and the empaths in the corporate world who felt crushed by the pressures from toxic work cultures and unfulfilling work. Initially, the audience consisted of my brother and a handful of friends, with only occasional interactions from random strangers who would occasionally leave a "like" or two. I reminded myself that it would be worth it if I could help just one person reading my content.

Then, an unexpected and remarkable turn of events unfolded. One of my posts garnered an astonishing 30,000 likes and was viewed by hundreds of thousands.

Gradually, the community burgeoned, encompassing hundreds of thousands of individuals from around the globe. Today, over 10 million people actively engage with my content each year. Messages poured in from people who shared how my posts had pulled them back from the brink of despair or provided the strength to persevere when they felt utterly defeated. It became clear that my words struck a resonant chord, particularly with those often marginalized—the underdogs grappling with racism, sexism, classism, and ableism within the toxic crucible of corporate culture. It dawned on me that I had the potential to serve those who felt continually beaten down, a sentiment I had experienced firsthand throughout my corporate journey as a perpetual outcast.

My venture, the Community of Seven, reached new heights. I launched bi-weekly free trainings that I packaged into Microlearnings and Let's Talk with the goal of training over a million people worldwide. We reached people throughout the world from Kenya to Manila to Des Moines. Those talks turned into a YouTube channel. Invitations to speak at events worldwide and inquiries from companies seeking my expertise in team training became a regular occurrence. In addition to my online presence, I compiled my most stirring posts into the book you now hold in your hands.

Little did I foresee that a simple weekly call would propel me into a position where I could impact the lives of millions. Such is the magic that unfolds when you listen to your core values. Once you align with your true purpose, your capacity to effect positive change in the world expands exponentially.

Quotes: A Shortcut to Life's Biggest Lessons

The foundation of my social media posts has always been rooted in a familiar format, a tradition from my childhood that holds a deep significance.

As Vietnamese refugees, our household lacked material abundance, but we possessed a cherished, well-worn book of quotes by renowned leaders and authors. My father, a man of few words, would select quotes for discussion, and those moments became treasured memories. Little did I realize that this childhood ritual would profoundly shape my future.

Fast forward three decades, and I returned to this familiar habit. I began selecting quotes that resonated with me, crafting posts that expounded on the wisdom encapsulated within these succinct phrases. Quotes possess a unique power—they can convey profound insights, encapsulate intricate ideas, and ignite inspiration. They serve as poignant reminders of the wisdom deep within our hearts and minds, waiting to be awakened. It's worth noting that I have made every effort to attribute each quote accurately. However, the origins of quotes can often be challenging to trace, and they may be shared and attributed to various sources over time. In cases where the source remains unknown, I will duly note it as such.

The format of each lesson in this book mirrors this structure: a thought-provoking quote followed by a reflection. I've also included exercises designed to enable you to apply these lessons immediately. Did I mention I once was a teacher? So yes, I'm giving you homework. These exercises are brief and accessible, requiring nothing more than a journal and an open mind, taking ten minutes or less to complete. I promise you if you do these exercises daily, your life will transform. I have done these same exercises with leaders from across the globe including CEOs, Fortune 500 executives and yes, even myself.

It has always been my goal to democratize training and development, it is the only way we can create systemic equality in the world. Knowledge should not be gatekept by those with power, money or esteemed degrees.

Feel free to dive into this book at your leisure. Whether you enjoy reading it cover to cover or simply want inspiration and guidance whenever you like. The choice is yours!

The book is organized into four distinct sections, each addressing crucial facets of personal growth:

1. What Matters Most:

    Prioritizing what truly matters. Delve into the exploration of your true purpose and start living your values as your North Star. Contemplate the person you aspire to become.

2. Your Mindset Creates Your Destiny:

    Learn the art of cultivating a mindset that propels you toward your purpose.

3. Change Requires Consistent Action:

    Take the initial steps to align your actions with your authentic self. Transformation requires consistent action. We become what we do daily.

4. Change Requires Changing Who We Are.

    The art of becoming requires that we change and let go of what we are no longer. Develop consistency in both your mindset and actions. Embrace the practice of living your purpose daily and inspire others to do the same.

Remember that the journey toward becoming your true self is fueled by four essential ingredients: the right purpose, the right mindset, the right actions, and the right community. These elements together pave the path to becoming the person you were destined to be.

We Are All Students and Teachers

Here's the thing: I'm not a guru. I'm not telling you anything you don't already know. I'm not an influencer and have no desire to be one.

What I am is a teacher and also a student. We are all students, and we are simultaneously teachers. You cannot teach if you're not also a passionate learner. And the best way to learn is through teaching.

My mission is to remind you of what you should already know: you are stronger than any of your challenges, and you have the power to do great things. You also have the capability to do hard things. Never forget that you were put on this earth to find your purpose and to live it. Never forget how amazing you are; now fix your crown—we got the world to conquer and people to help.

Illustration: Morgan Messam. This is a drawing of the original community of seven as drawn by my daughter Morgan who was 5-years-old at the time. In the picture: Lan, Morgan, Rachel, Delaney, Natalie, Sarah and Claudine.

FIX YOUR CROWN

Kings and queens,
straighten your crown.
Stand tall and proud.
Walk through the world like
you matter, for indeed, you do.
Though some may try, no
one can take your dignity,
determination, and drive.
What's meant for you,
will always be yours.

DO THIS
DAILY

SECRET 1

WHAT MATTERS MOST

Prioritizing What Truly Matters:
Discovering Your North Star

What Matters Most?

This seemingly simple question possesses the transformative power to reshape your entire life. Sadly, many of us never take a moment to pause and truly contemplate the answer. Instead, we often tread the well-worn path or inherit the dreams and desires of our parents, peers, or the prevailing popular opinion.

Consider the story of a CEO I had the privilege of working with. She had recently departed from her high-profile position at a renowned Fortune 100 brand. Her aspirations involved starting her own business and spending more quality time with her family. However, when an old colleague suggested she was too young to "retire," insinuating that her entrepreneurial venture amounted to giving up, she began to doubt herself. In that moment of doubt, I posed a pivotal question: 'What is it that you truly want?' She confided in me, expressing her desire to breathe freely, to be present with her family, to indulge in 2 p.m. yoga sessions, and to revel in the sweet embrace of freedom. I then asked her the critical follow-up: 'If that's what you genuinely desire, would returning to the corporate world fulfill any of those aspirations?' Her response was a resounding 'no.'

How many of us are leading lives that conform to the expectations of others? How often do we make decisions not based on our actual desires but instead on what we believe success should look like in the eyes of family, society, or colleagues? We can only connect the dots in our lives once we can articulate our core values and identify what truly brings us happiness.

Far too often, we delay our happiness and stifle our desires, waiting for the 'perfect time.' But what happens when we suppress our deepest yearnings? To borrow the words of Langston Hughes, "What happens to a dream deferred?" What transpires when we fail to articulate what truly matters to us?

Bonnie Ware, in her book *The Top Five Regrets of the Dying*, shares profound insights gleaned from years of interviewing patients in the twilight of their lives as a palliative nurse. She asserts that people attain a remarkable clarity of vision when they know their time is limited. She further contends that we can glean wisdom from their experiences. "When questioned about any regrets they had or anything they would do differently,' she notes, 'one of the most common regrets was, "I wish I'd had the courage to live a life true to myself, not the life others expected of me."' This poignant revelation underscores the profound impact of living in alignment with our genuine desires and values."

Consider this: if you cannot pinpoint what holds the utmost importance in your life, how can you ever hope to lead a life that authentically reflects who you are? Spoiler alert: you can't.

Core Values: What Matters Most?

Life operates much like a GPS navigation system. To reach your desired destination, you must input a specific address. In life, that address is intentionality—an unwavering understanding of what truly matters to you. It's about translating that understanding into your core values and living them in every facet of your existence. However, the critical first step is to discern what genuinely matters to you. Without this clarity, finding your purpose in life becomes an elusive quest.

Your core values and your purpose are intrinsically linked. Your core values provide the foundation to discern and define your purpose. In turn, your purpose imbues your core values with meaning and direction. When these two aspects align harmoniously, you can live authentically, experiencing life on a profound level—a life driven by purpose.

Once we discover our core values, they become our guiding principles that help us navigate various aspects of our lives. They provide the moral and ethical compass that directs our lives and decision-making.

We are all placed on this earth with a unique purpose and a distinct calling. Our journey in life involves the discovery of this individual purpose and the 'why' behind it. Once you can identify your core values, the next step is to live your life based on those values. To live your values as if they were your North Star.

Discovering Your North Star

In astronomy and navigation, the North Star, known as Polaris, is a prominent star close to the celestial north pole. Due to its fixed position relative to Earth's rotation, the North Star has been used for centuries as a reliable navigational reference point by Wayfinders, those skilled in traditional navigation methods.

And like its astronomical counterpart, one's North Star, metaphorically, represents your guiding principle or purpose in life. It symbolizes the direction you want to take based on your deepest values and what truly matters most to you.

Just as sailors use the North Star as a constant reference point to guide their journey, finding your personal North Star means identifying your life's purpose and the principles that guide your decisions and actions. Your North Star is your inner compass for navigating life's journey. It represents your ultimate life goals and aspirations, giving you a clear direction to follow.

Core values and your North Star are closely related because they both play a significant role in guiding your life, decisions, and actions. Where your North Star often embodies your overarching purpose or the direction you want to take in life, your core values are the fundamental principles and beliefs that matter most to you. When your core values align with your North Star, your actions and choices are consistent with your deeper sense of purpose.

My Search for Meaning and Finding My North Star

Although I didn't start uncovering genuine answers until late in life, the quest for my 'why' has been a lifelong journey. My life took a profound turn during my college years while studying Psychology at Stanford University when I encountered Viktor Frankl's *Man's Search for Meaning.*

Frankl's harrowing survival story from the Holocaust led him to establish Logotherapy, a branch of psychology centered on discovering one's life's purpose as a means not only to thrive but, in extreme cases, to endure.

Born into the tumultuous world as a refugee escaping war-torn Vietnam and raised in poverty in Los Angeles, California, I grew up amid an atmosphere fraught with trauma—poverty, gang violence, racism, and despair. As a result, I carried a heavy burden of anger and resentment throughout my youth.

I often questioned why life had dealt me such a challenging hand. At age 13, I tragically lost a friend to gang violence. By the time I turned 17, I was supporting myself financially. The weight of losing my father bore down on me at 19.

Frankl's words awakened a profound realization: I wasn't merely a victim of my circumstances; I held the power to shape my destiny. It was in the space between the traumas I had endured and my responses where my true strength resided. It became evident that I had a choice—an agency I owned and controlled.

Life was not happening 'to' me; it was happening 'for' me. While I couldn't control the external events that unfolded in my life, my power was harnessed through my response to them. Furthermore, I understood that I had a purpose on this earth, a duty to unearth it and that this quest was inextricably linked to answering my 'why.'

Your Journey Begins Now, Raindrops

As you dive into the forthcoming content, I wish you to embark on a journey of self-discovery and unearth your true purpose. Our journey commences on the following page. Initially, I will assist you in recognizing something you already hold within: you are capable of anything you put your mind to, but it starts with the belief that you can. You are the ideal individual to embark on this transformative journey, and the present moment is precisely the right time to commence.

Following this first lesson, I will lead you to explore your core values, empowering you to pursue your distinctive purpose across all aspects of your life. Once you've discovered your core values, ensure they become your North Star—that your actions and choices are consistent with your deeper sense of purpose.

I've found that when you truly begin living your values, the universe opens, and miracles start unfolding. Remember the story I shared earlier about being laid off from Fortune Magazine at the start of the pandemic? Instead of building a startup for them, I launched my company, Community of Seven in six months. Sometimes, rejection is redirection propelling us towards our purpose. Your North Star, shaped by your values, illuminates you with a clear direction to follow on your path to becoming your authentic self.

"Our core values are the guiding stars illuminating our path, shaping who we are and how we want to impact the world. At its core, our values hold the answer to life's most profound question: 'What matters to me?'"

–Lan Phan

IDENTIFY YOUR CORE VALUES

Understanding our core values isn't just a valuable life lesson; it's an essential ingredient to self-discovery and happiness. However, it's not just about identifying our values but embodying them daily.

When our core values seamlessly integrate into our decision-making process, they transform into our unwavering North Star. This guiding light leads us towards discovering our higher self and enables us to discern the meaningful contributions we can offer to the world.

Once we align with our core values, it's about moving closer each day to who we were born to be. We will have hurdles to overcome, but our life accelerates in ways unknown as long we keep moving forward.

Remember, your journey starts with that first step—identifying your core values and using them as your North Star to help you navigate your life decisions.

💡 Exercise: Unearth Your Core Values

This exercise is designed to help you identify and clarify your core values—the guiding principles that define what truly matters to you. By uncovering these values and ranking them in order of significance, you can better understand your life's priorities and aspirations.

Identify Your Top Ten Priorities:

- Take some time to contemplate and list the ten most important things in your life.
- Write a brief description or reason why each item on your list is significant to you.

What Makes Your Soul Sing:

- Review your list and identify common themes or recurring elements among your top ten priorities.
- Select the key themes that resonate the most with your heart and evoke a profound sense of fulfillment.

Define Your Core Values:

- Based on the themes you've identified, create concise core values that encapsulate your deepest beliefs and desires. For example, if helping others is a recurring theme, one of your core values could be "Service to Others." If adventure and exploration are central, your core value might be "Travel and Adventure."
- Craft one or more core values that align with your identified themes. Write these down in your journal.

Rank Your Core Values:

- Once you've defined your core values, arrange them in rank order of importance to you. Begin with the value that holds the greatest significance at the top, followed by the next most important, and so on.
- This activity is essential when our values clash. For example, if your two values are family and travel. Taking a solo world trip for a year and not seeing your family for that period would conflict. Understanding how your core values rank will help guide you when there is a conflict of priorities.
- Take your time to contemplate and prioritize your values based on how strongly they resonate with your life's vision.

Reflect on Your Insights:

- Consider the significance of your ranked core values. Reflect on how they can guide your decision-making and actions in various aspects of your life.
- Write down any insights or realizations from this exercise and how you might apply your core values to lead a more fulfilling life.

Living Your Core Values:

- Commit to integrating your core values into your daily life. When you can do this, they become your North Star. Consider aligning your choices and actions with these values to foster a sense of purpose and fulfillment.
- Regularly revisit and refine your core values as your life evolves, ensuring they align with your aspirations and beliefs.

By delving into your core values and prioritizing them, you'll understand what truly matters to you. This exercise serves as a valuable compass, helping you navigate life's choices and decisions in alignment with your deepest beliefs and desires.

MY NORTH STAR

"Allow Your Goals, Dreams, Values and Purpose to Guide You."
—Lan Phan

What matters most to you? What's the principle that guides you?

My North Star has always been my family, particularly my daughter. When I've contemplated giving up or, even worse, not even trying, focusing on what matters most helps me reaffirm my purpose and resolve.

During periods of dwindling motivation, I carry a photograph of my daughter in my wallet as a reminder to persevere. All it takes is a glance to remind me of my North Star and why giving up is not an option.

When times get tough, remind yourself of your purpose, "why," and reason for being. That will become your North Star when times get tough.

You will run into challenges. But remember, your purpose is more significant than any obstacle standing in your way.

💡 Exercise: Discovering Your North Star

- Visualize a clear night sky filled with stars. Imagine one star shining brighter and more brilliantly than the others. This star represents your purpose, your "why."
- Focus on the guiding star and think about what truly matters to you. Refer to your Core Values in the exercise prior. It could be your family, personal growth, a career goal, a passion, or a cause you deeply care about.
- Feel the warmth and energy radiating from this star. Let it fill you with purpose, motivation, and unwavering consistency.
- Reflect on moments when your sense of purpose has driven you to overcome challenges or take essential actions. Recall the emotions and determination you felt during those times.

- Now, consider a current challenge or goal you're facing. Imagine how your North Star and purpose can light the way and guide you through this situation.
- Open your eyes and take a moment to journal your thoughts. Write down your purpose and why it matters to you. Describe how it can serve as your North Star during tough times.
- Whenever you encounter difficulties or lack motivation, return to this visualization and remind yourself of your North Star. Let it reignite your sense of purpose and provide the strength to push through obstacles.

GROW WILDLY

*"Like wildflowers, you must allow yourself to grow in
all the places people thought you never would."*
—E.V. Rogina.

I spent too much of my life focused on people-pleasing, caring excessively about others' opinions, and harboring crippling self-doubt.

The transformation towards growth and living an authentic life was made possible once I was able to do the following:

- Embrace my core values.
- Make daily decisions that are congruent with my core values.
- Exercise self-discipline with my time and energy.
- Challenge and rewrite my limiting beliefs.
- Surround myself with those who share my values.

Don't get me wrong: I'm not saying growth is easy. It's not. It's challenging and often painful. It's a journey without end that demands time, dedication, and profound self-reflection.

But you know what?

Repeat after me:
The journey is worth it.
I am worth it.

We deserve to live the life of our dreams and embark on a path of wild and unimaginable growth.

This is my time to manifest my dreams and flourish abundantly. Repeat after me, "Like wildflowers, watch me grow where people said I couldn't."

💡 **Exercise: Take a moment to reflect on your life and journey toward authenticity. Consider the following steps as a guide to explore your growth and authenticity:**

- List the values that resonate most with you. These could be values like honesty, kindness, family, adventure, or any other principles that hold personal significance.
- Reflect on your daily decisions and actions. Are they aligned with your core values? Identify instances where you felt in harmony with your values and moments when you veered away from them.
- Examine your daily routine and time management. Are you dedicating time to the things that truly matter to you, or are you caught up in activities that drain your energy and don't align with your values?
- Think about any beliefs or thoughts that have held you back. These could be doubts about your abilities or negative self-talk. Challenge these limiting beliefs and consider how they've influenced your decisions.
- Evaluate your social circle. Are you surrounded by people who share your values and support your growth? Identify relationships that uplift you and those that may be hindering your authenticity.
- Create a plan for your growth journey. Define specific actions you can take to align your life more closely with your core values. Set achievable goals and milestones.
- Journal about your experiences and insights as you embark on this journey toward authenticity. Note any challenges you face and the progress you make.

Remember, the path to living authentically is a continuous process. Be patient with yourself and celebrate the small victories along the way. Your growth is worth the effort, and you have the power to shape your authentic life.

GIVE YOURSELF ATTENTION

"The greatest gift that you can give yourself is
a little bit of your own attention."
—Anthony J. D'Angelo.

Allow yourself the freedom to make mistakes. Extend to yourself the same love and care you generously offer to others.

Grant yourself the gift of restful, rejuvenating sleep each night. Provide your body with nourishing, wholesome food that fuels your well-being.

Create a safe, supportive space for your healing and growth. Foster a work environment that nurtures your spirit instead of depleting it.

Practice patience and self-compassion in your journey.

Embrace courage and faith, empowering yourself to overcome any obstacles that may cross your path.

Surround yourself with friends who uplift and inspire you.

Embrace the transformative journey of introspection as a precious gift to yourself.

💡 Exercise: Clarify Your Priorities and Optimize Your Time

This exercise is designed to help you gain clarity on your values, aspirations, and time management while eliminating time-wasting activities.

- Take some time to ponder what genuinely matters to you. Consider your values, long-term goals, and personal aspirations. Write them down to create a clear vision of your goal and experience.
- Now, focus on identifying time-wasting elements in your life. These activities or habits drain your time and energy without providing significant value or joy. Examples could include excessive

social media use, prolonged TV watching, unproductive meetings, or toxic relationships.

- Conduct a time audit for a few days or even a week. Record your daily activities and how you spend your time. This will provide you with an accurate picture of where your time is going and highlight areas that need improvement.
- Once you've completed your time audit, review it in the context of your priorities and values. Identify tasks and activities that align with your goals and values. These are the high-priority tasks that contribute to your objectives.
- Prioritize the tasks and activities that align with your goals and values. Consider delegating or eliminating lower-priority functions that do not contribute significantly to your objectives—delegate where possible to free up time for higher-value activities.

By following these steps, you'll better understand your priorities and how you spend your time. This will enable you to optimize your time management, focus on what truly matters, and work toward your most important goals and aspirations.

"When you stop pursuing what no longer serves you, you open the door for the right things to find you. Make room for blessings."

–Lan Phan

ASK THE RIGHT QUESTIONS

No one is on their deathbed wishing they had logged more hours in the office. Nobody.

Your legacy isn't defined by what you own.

When I stand at heaven's gate, I'm confident God won't be evaluating my CV, LinkedIn profile, or Instagram likes. God won't care what Ivy League school I went to.

So why do we spend so much of our lives chasing things that don't matter? Why do we obsess over others' opinions? Why do we tether our worth to our bank balances?

Stop caring about things that aren't important.

We spend too much of our lives chasing things because society tells us they hold value. Instead, ask:

What truly matters to *you*?
What brings you joy?
What impact do I want to make in the world?
How do you wish to spend *your* precious time on Earth?
When you ask the right questions, the answers will come.

💡 Exercise: Discovering What Matters

This exercise aims to prompt introspection by brainstorming answers to essential life questions.

Reflect on Life's Significance; begin by contemplating the following questions:

- What truly matters to you?
- What activities or experiences bring you genuine joy?

- What kind of impact do you aspire to make in the world during your lifetime?
- How do you envision spending your precious time on Earth to lead a fulfilling life?

Start writing down your responses to these questions without filtering or censoring your thoughts. Don't worry about grammar, structure, or coherence; simply allow your ideas to flow freely. Dive deep into your thoughts and feelings as you explore your values, passions, and aspirations. Write down anything that comes to mind, even if it seems unconventional or unexpected.

Take a moment to review what you've written. Reflect on your responses and consider how they align with your current life and aspirations. Based on your brainstorming, identify critical values, sources of joy, aspirations, and ways you wish to spend your time. Prioritize these elements and set intentions for incorporating them into your life.

This exercise is a starting point for clarifying what truly matters to you. It can help you better understand your core values and provide direction for making choices that align with your authentic self.

"In the pursuit of making a living, don't forget to create a life worth living. Remember, you are not your job. And while you may be replaceable at work, your role at home isn't. Home is what matters."

–Lan Phan

YOU ARE NOT YOUR WORK

Throughout my life, I relentlessly pursued empty titles, promotions, and commendations. I would scour job listings and opportunities based on these superficial markers and mold my life around my work. Unfortunately, after enduring twelve-hour workdays, there wasn't much left when I finally got home.

But today, my perspective has shifted. I've reordered my priorities to focus on what truly matters to me:

- My family (including the friends who have become my chosen family).
- Faith (nurturing my relationship with God).
- Helping people (dedicating myself to serving others).
- Freedom (taking charge of my destiny by starting my own business).

Gone are the days of chasing after workplace accolades. Instead, I've homed in on what brings me genuine happiness and fulfillment. My core values now serve as my guiding principles, shaping the very foundation of my business.

For instance, I spent 80 percent of my time traveling in my previous roles. When I constructed my own business, I deliberately designed a structure that allowed me to reduce travel by taking on virtual clients. Even when I travel for speaking engagements, I often bring my husband and daughter to ensure I'm not sacrificing precious family time.

Moreover, as I built my company, I envisioned a business that could assist those who couldn't afford my services. This led me to launch a YouTube channel offering free content to help a wider audience. My paid corporate training and keynote speaking fees help fund my non-paid services.

And when times get rough, which they often do, I repeat my mantra: In the relentless pursuit of earning a living, always remember to build a life worth living.

♥ Exercise: What are your most important core values?

Take a moment to reflect on your own life. Consider the values and principles that truly matter to you. Identify three core values that resonate with your soul and give you deep fulfillment.

Now, think about your current job or career. Does it align with these core values? Are there aspects of your work that conflict with what matters most to you in life? Write down your thoughts on this matter.

Next, envision how to restructure your career or job to align with your core values. What changes can you make, even small ones, to create harmony between your work and your values? List at least three actionable steps to bring about this alignment.

Remember, there is always time to reprioritize and create a life worth living. This exercise is a step toward aligning your career with what truly matters to you.

YOUR POSSESSIONS DON'T DEFINE YOU

"In our society, we buy things we don't need, with money we don't have, to impress people we don't even like. Let's just stop that."
—Dave Ramsey.

As people near the end of their lives, no one is on their deathbed wishing they had more things. Their reflections usually center on something other than acquiring more possessions or accumulating wealth. Instead, they reflect on the life they've lived.

They gather their loved ones, cherishing those near and far.

They regret opportunities lost. They think of words unspoken.

They wish they had lived the life they wanted rather than one defined by external expectations.

Ask yourself: Are you dedicating your time to building a life you can genuinely be proud of, or are you trapped in a cycle of work and financial stress, all so you can buy more things to impress people you don't even know or like.

Shift your priorities, and you'll transform your life.

💡 Exercise: Look around your home and identify three items you've purchased but now regret or rarely use.

Why did you feel compelled to buy them, and what needs or desires were you trying to fulfill then? What are the things in your house collecting dust, and what can you learn from that purchase? I still have that bag and don't use it, preferring to use swag canvas bags I get from conferences.

"Embrace today, for tomorrow is not promised. Live each moment as a gift because it genuinely is.

We get one chance to live the life of our wildest dreams.

Don't squander it."

–Lan Phan

MAKE EACH DAY COUNT

Live each day with purpose, for tomorrow is not promised. How often do we squander away valuable moments in needless worry, carrying the weight of guilt and resentment, all while our dreams gradually slip through our grasp. What might your life become if you were to actively pursue your dreams?

Life is short.
Stop worrying about trivial things.

How would you live if your time was limited?
What if you had only a few years? A few months? A few days?

I hope you won't squander those precious moments of fretting, comparing, grumbling, craving, and yearning.

Instead, I hope you'll fill your days with gratitude, prayer, love, ambition, and accomplishment.

Life comes with an expiration date. Embrace each day and make it count. Thread those days together into purposeful weeks and those weeks into joyful months, crafting a life worth celebrating.

💡 Exercise: The Gift of Time Perspective

In your journal, reflect on these questions:

- How would you shape your life if you knew you had only five years left?
- What about if you had just one year?
- How about a few months?
- Lastly, imagine you had only a few days.

Visualize your daily activities, your relationships, and how you'd spend your precious time.

Too often, we meander through life as if it's an endless journey. This exercise encourages you to picture your life with urgency.

DON'T SETTLE

"Ten years from now, make sure you can say that
you chose your life, you didn't settle for it."
—Mandy Hale.

Embrace the miracle of life.

Life is a miraculous gift. Yet, many of us unintentionally undervalue it by settling for less. We settle for relationships that do not fulfill us. We consume food that does not nourish our bodies. We endure jobs that bring us no joy. We neglect ourselves, often failing to show the kindness we deserve.

Let me remind you that the fact that you are breathing in itself is a miracle. So, why do you treat your life as anything less than extraordinary? Why do you allow yourself to settle?

Why do you doubt yourself?

You were put on this earth for a reason.

You are a child of God.

As kids, we dreamt big. Think back to your childhood when you dreamed without limits. You aspired to be astronauts, presidents, and Olympic athletes. Yet, as the years passed, those dreams often lost their grandiosity and became diluted. You began to settle.

But here's the truth: there is always time to reignite those dreams. Chase your dreams till they become your reality.

Live a great life. Live your purpose, and don't squander the extraordinary blessing that is your life. Don't waste the gift.

💡 Exercise: Rekindle Your Dreams

- Recall your childhood dreams and ambitions. What did you aspire to become or achieve when you were young? Write down at least three of these dreams.

- Next, consider how and why these dreams became less prominent as you grew older. What circumstances or beliefs led you to settle for less? Be honest with yourself and jot down your thoughts.

- Now, consider which of these childhood dreams still resonate with you today. Find the kernel of truth in those dreams. For example, if you wanted to be a Clown, perhaps the truth is that you have a passion for entertaining and making people laugh. Are there any that, deep down, you still long to pursue? Circle or highlight these dreams.

- For each circled dream, write down one small, actionable step you can take next week to rekindle your pursuit of it. It could be as simple as doing online research, contacting a mentor, or signing up for a relevant class or workshop.

- Commit to taking those steps within the next seven days, no matter how small.

- As you embark on this journey to reignite your dreams, remind yourself daily of the miraculous gift that is life. Use this reminder to fuel your determination and ensure you never settle.

This exercise will help you reconnect with your childhood dreams and take the initial steps toward making them a reality.

CHOOSE TO LIVE A REMARKABLE LIFE

"Live your life in such a way that if you die at 99,
it's still too soon."
—Anonymous

When we think of Betty White, who passed away at age 99, we can draw valuable lessons from her remarkable life. Let's strive to embody her essence by embracing these principles:

- Be unapologetically and authentically yourself.
- Cultivate kindness while maintaining your inner strength.
- Never, let age or obstacles stagnate your personal growth.
- Recognize that your value increases as you continue to age.
- Embrace change and reinvent yourself as needed.
- Face challenges with poise and a smile.
- Advocate for others.
- Be unapologetically and authentically yourself.

May we live so thoroughly that, when we take our final breaths, we can look back without regrets and say, "Wasn't that an incredible life."

💡 Exercise: Envision Your Dream Life

Take a moment to picture yourself at the end of your life, reflecting on your incredible journey. As you look back, imagine the life of your dreams, which fills you with joy and fulfillment. Visualize this ideal life in vivid detail. Now, open your journal and dedicate ten minutes to describing this dream life in writing. Let your imagination flow freely and paint a rich, detailed picture of the life you aspire to live.

CHOOSE TO BE INSPIRED

*"I am learning every day to allow the space between
where I want to be and where I am to inspire me and not terrify me."*
—Tracee Ellis Ross.

Growth is scary;
It means taking risks.
It means betting on yourself.
It means learning something new.
It means trying something new.
It means becoming who you were meant to be.

The unknown can be scary, but don't let it make you live a small life. You were made to live a big life. Embrace the potential for greatness that resides deep within you. Live your definition of "big"—even if it means living a simple life.

What does living your best life look like? Define and imagine it so you can visualize it daily and, more importantly, take the necessary steps and action to get there. The growth needed to achieve your dreams is the space between where you are today and where you need to be.

You can approach this journey with either fear or excitement; choose one.

💡 Exercise: Create Your Vision and Embrace Growth

Take a moment to picture your ideal life vividly. What does it look like? Create a quick vision board, or simply jot down your thoughts.

Now, consider what steps you need to take to align with your ideal life. What books can you read? What people should you connect with? What training is required? What lifestyle changes are needed to bridge the gap between your current self and your ideal self?

Embrace each of these actions with excitement and enthusiasm. Remember, every step you take brings you closer to your best life."

TUNE OUT THE NOISE

"And Every day, the world will drag you by the hand, yelling, 'This is important! And this is important! You need to worry about this! And This! And This!' And each day, it's up to you to yank your hand back, put it on your heart, and say, 'No. This is what's important.'"
—Iaian Thomas

Living a life of purpose and authenticity can be difficult in a world constantly demanding our attention. Society is designed to make us believe we're lacking, pushing us to fill that void with material possessions, indulgence, and unhealthy distractions.

The message bombarding us is clear:
You are incomplete.
You need this. You need me.
Look at this. Buy this.

Let me stand here and gently remind you:
You are whole.
You are enough.
You are complete.
You are beautiful just as you are.

In a world that thrives on making us feel inadequate, driving us to consume more and work harder in an unending cycle, the ability to tune out the noise and focus on what truly matters is nothing short of revolutionary.

💡 **Exercise: Repeat this mantra when you awake and before you go to bed, "I AM ENOUGH."**

"Claim your place in this world. You belong. Don't settle for a small life when you deserve to occupy space. Manspread, if necessary, take up every inch you need, my dear. The world needs what you got. Never underestimate your worth for anyone, understood?"

–Lan Phan

DREAM BIG, AUDACIOUS DREAMS

Never be afraid to live a big life.
It takes courage to believe in yourself.
It takes courage to see your greatness.
So, bet on yourself, even when others won't.

Dream big.
Work hard.
Be kind.
Serve.

Stop living a small life.
Stop listening to the naysayers.
Some will doubt you; don't you be one of them.

Embrace the courage to believe in yourself and your potential.

See your light.

Success will inevitably follow, for life expands to match the size of your dreams.

The universe rewards those who believe in themselves and act accordingly.

TAKE CONTROL OF YOUR STORY

"Trust the next chapter because you are the author."
—Unknown

We can't control what life throws at us, but we can control how we respond to those situations.

If you find yourself dissatisfied with the current narrative of your life, remember that you possess the power to redefine it.

You can append an additional chapter, include an appendix, or rewrite the whole book if necessary.

Embrace this creative authority and start crafting the narrative that resonates most deeply with your aspirations and dreams.

You are the author of your story. You always have been.

💡 Exercise: Reimagine Your Story

Reflect on your life's story. Are there aspects that no longer align with your aspirations, values, or desires? Identify any chapters or elements that you wish to rewrite or revise. Next, envision the story you'd like to create. What would the ideal narrative of your life look like? How would you want it to unfold? What new chapters, experiences, or achievements do you envision? Commit to making the necessary changes to bring your desired story to life. Whether taking small steps or embarking on a significant transformation, remember that you hold the authorship of your story. Start rewriting your narrative today.

LIVE INTENTIONALLY

"Make a list of things that make you happy.
Make a list of things you do every day.
Compare the lists.
Adjust accordingly."
—Murray Newlands

One of life's most transformative lessons revolves around the profound impact of intentionality—the deliberate and purposeful act of steering your energy toward your desired destinations. For anything you genuinely crave in life, intentionality is the compass that points the way.

Think of intentionality as an address you input into a GPS. With a clear and precise address, your journey proceeds smoothly, guiding you precisely to your destination.

However, if your address is vague or incorrect, you'll encounter numerous detours, some fraught with hazards and winding roads, potentially preventing you from reaching your desired endpoint.

Intentionality serves as a guiding force, illuminating what holds significance for you. It directs you toward your purpose and aligns you with the grander vision you have for yourself. Moreover, it activates cognitive processes that heighten your awareness of opportunities to propel you toward your goals and, ultimately, your dream life.

💡 Exercise: Cultivating Daily Happiness

Today, let's embark on an impactful exercise:

- Begin by crafting a list of the things that genuinely bring you happiness and fulfillment.
- Simultaneously, compile a list of your daily activities and routines.
- Now, it's time to compare these two lists, examining how closely your daily life aligns with the sources of your happiness.

- With this newfound awareness, take proactive steps to adjust your daily routines and activities accordingly. Ensure that your days are infused with the elements that genuinely bring you joy and contentment.

This exercise serves as a compass to navigate your daily life toward a more fulfilling and happier existence.

DIG DEEP

"Go within every day and find the inner strength so that the world will not blow your candle out."
—Katherine Dunham

Dig deep.
Unleash your unseen strength inside of you.
Deep within you lies a reservoir of strength beyond your wildest dreams.

You are stronger than you can ever imagine. You standing here today is a testament to your indomitable spirit.

The pain you've endured and the challenges you've faced were always meant to strengthen you, not weaken you.

You've faced hardships and have the scars to prove it. But never forget, scar tissue has always been tougher than undamaged skin.

Your trial and tribulation have strengthened you. It has chiseled you into who you are and equipped you for the next chapter of your journey.

Embrace the growth, keep moving forward, and never underestimate the incredible strength that resides deep within you.

💡 Exercise: Embracing Your Scars of Strength

Take a moment to focus on your body and its unique story. Gently look at the scars on your skin, whether small or significant, old or new. As you observe each imperfection, touch them with care. Feel the texture beneath your fingertips. Let your mind linger on the positive and challenging memories associated with these marks.

Recognize that each scar represents a moment when you faced adversity, a trial, or a challenging experience—After the pain came healing. These moments may have been tough, but they have also contributed to your resilience and growth.

Inhale deeply, embracing the idea that your scars are symbols of your inner strength. They are evidence of your ability to endure and overcome. Remember that just like scar tissue is tougher than unblemished skin, you have become stronger through your trials and tribulations.

Affirm your resilience by saying aloud or in your mind: "I am stronger because of my scars. They are a testament to my inner fortitude."

Take a moment to appreciate your body for its resilience and your scars as markers of your journey.

Whenever you encounter self-doubt or face new challenges, return to this exercise. Your scars are constant reminders of your strength and your ability to overcome.

This exercise encourages you to honor and embrace your physical and emotional scars, recognizing them as badges of resilience and growth rather than imperfections.

RECOGNIZE YOUR INHERENT WORTH

"Your progress does not need to be seen or validated by other people."
—Unknown.

It took me quite some time to internalize this essential truth: The power to validate my worth resides solely with God, my ancestor, and "me, myself & I."

This precious right belongs to me and me alone.

Every step of progress I make, I fully embrace.
Every stumble and fall, I accept with grace.
My intrinsic value, I cherish.

In my younger days, I contorted and shapeshifted, desperately seeking acceptance. I remember the sting of a negative performance review from a boss who failed to recognize my contributions. Similarly, I felt the pain of heartbreak when certain relationships faltered. In response, I masked my true self and bent to fit others' expectations.

Let me be the one to tell you that doing your job and life is hard enough without having to pretend to be someone else. Not everyone will like or appreciate you, and that's okay. It's their loss. If they can't see how amazing you are, walk away. Run.

I've said it before, and I'll repeat it for those who need to hear it: their inability to recognize your worth does not diminish it. No one can take away your intrinsic value.

Stop letting others dictate your happiness and self-worth. Period. End of story.

Your worth is immeasurable, and it's high time you recognize it yourself.

💡 Exercise: Claiming Your Self-Worth

Identify External Validation: Consider instances in your life when you sought external validation or changed yourself to be accepted by others. These could be work situations, personal relationships, or any other aspect of your life. Write down a few examples.

Remind yourself that your worth is not contingent on the validation or approval of others. Reflect on the idea that your progress, setbacks, and values are yours to acknowledge and embrace. Jot down your thoughts and feelings.

Think about the lessons you've learned from past experiences where you sought validation from others and felt the need to conform. What insights can you draw from these moments? Write them down.

Embrace the notion that your worth is immeasurable and unique. Repeat the affirmation, "My worth is inherent and immeasurable."

Visualize yourself, releasing the need for external validation and the burden of trying to fit others' expectations. Imagine a weight being lifted off your shoulders, leaving you feeling lighter and freer.

Create a list of positive affirmations related to your self-worth. For example, "I am worthy just as I am," "I value myself regardless of others' opinions," or "My worth is unwavering."

Incorporate these affirmations into your daily routine. Repeat them to yourself each morning or whenever you encounter self-doubt.

This exercise is designed to help you recognize and affirm your inherent self-worth, letting go of the need for external validation. Acknowledging your value and uniqueness can build greater self-esteem and confidence in various aspects of your life.

FIND YOUR JOY

"I hope there are days when your coffee tastes like magic, your playlist makes you dance, strangers make you smile, and the night sky touches your soul. I hope you fall in love with being alive again."
—Brook Hampton.

As we strive to make a living, remember to make a life worth living. Your one job is crafting a life you would be proud of and a life worth cherishing.

What fills your heart with joy? If this question stumps you, make it your mission to uncover the answer.

Once you can vividly define and envision it, infuse your life with more of what sets your soul on fire.

And if you need some inspiration, just watch children. They instinctively know how to laugh and play. They possess an innate knack for laughter and play, continuously in pursuit of fun!

Watch their unbridled enthusiasm when they leap into puddles and dance in the rain. As adults, we must be conscious of our attempts to squash this spontaneity and zest for life.

When was the last time you actively pursued fun and adventure? Play more. Laugh more. Dance more. Remember, it's never too late to fall in love with life again.

💡 Exercise: Rediscovering Your Joy and Play

- Begin by setting aside some quiet time for self-reflection. Find a comfortable and peaceful place where you won't be disturbed.
- Take a few deep breaths to relax your mind and body. Close your eyes if it helps you concentrate.
- Think about your childhood and the activities or moments that brought you immense joy. What were the games you loved to play,

hobbies you were passionate about, or places you enjoyed visiting? Allow these memories to resurface.

- Open your journal or a blank piece of paper. List at least five childhood activities, hobbies, or experiences that brought you genuine joy and made you feel truly alive.
- Now, consider how many of these activities you've incorporated into your adult life. Have any of them fallen by the wayside as you've grown older?
- Select one activity from your list that you have not engaged in recently or have completely abandoned. Commit to reintroduce this activity into your life within the next week.
- Reflect on why this activity brought you joy in the past and how you can adapt it to your current circumstances.
- Visualize yourself engaging in this activity and feel the excitement and happiness it brings. Embrace the childlike enthusiasm you once had for it.
- Finally, set a specific date and time in your calendar to participate in this rediscovered joy. Make it a priority, and relish the experience when the day arrives.

This exercise is designed to help you reconnect with the activities that bring you joy and allow you to infuse more of that happiness into your adult life.

DO THE IMPOSSIBLE

"When someone tells you it can't be done, it's more a
reflection of their limitations, not yours."
—Unknown.

Scientists once thought the human body could never achieve the incredible feat of running a mile in under four minutes. It was considered too dangerous, too strenuous, and simply impossible. There were even fears that pushing the body to such limits could lead to catastrophic consequences; Some experts thought our body could explode if we pushed it to that limit.

However, in 1954, Roger Bannister shattered this once-unbreakable barrier, completing a mile in an astonishing three minutes and 59.4 seconds. His achievement opened the door for countless others. Since breaking this once-impossible feat, legions of others, including high-school runners, have run a mile in under four minutes.

This story reminds us that many things once deemed impossible have become reality:

- Flying
- Journeying to the moon
- Nanotechnology
- The Internet

Don't let other people's expectations of you become your ceiling in life. Not everyone will believe in you, and that's perfectly alright.

I wouldn't have done what I have, personally and professionally, if I had allowed the naysayers to dictate my path. Their skepticism merely reflects their own beliefs and constraints. The decision to believe them or not lies entirely within your control.

The choice is yours. Choose wisely.

💡 Exercise: Breaking Barriers

Reflect on when you faced skepticism or doubt from others about something you wanted to achieve or pursue. It could be a personal goal, a career aspiration, or a significant endeavor. Write down how you felt when confronted with this doubt or disbelief. Did it discourage you or motivate you to prove them wrong? Reflect on your initial response.

Now, think about the story of Roger Bannister and how he shattered the four-minute-mile barrier. How did he overcome the skepticism and disbelief of the scientific community? What qualities or mindset did he possess that enabled him to achieve the "impossible"? Consider the list of once-deemed-impossible achievements, such as flying or going to the moon. How did individuals or teams push beyond these limitations? What drove them to succeed?

Write down your aspirations and goals that others might have questioned or doubted. Consider adopting a mindset similar to those who achieved the "impossible" in various fields. Challenge yourself to set a new goal or milestone, even if it seems challenging or beyond your current capabilities. Use the stories of those who broke barriers as inspiration to pursue your dreams despite doubts or limitations.

Remember that the choice to believe in yourself and your abilities is entirely yours.

BE SPECIFIC

*"When praying for that job, also pray for a working environment
that won't lead you to burnout, depression, and regret."*
—Brigette Hyacinth.

One of the most profound life lessons I've learned is that you must be clear with what you want—whether it be how you live your life or your career choice.

During my early years, when it came to dating, I focused primarily on attraction and chemistry. I overlooked nuanced but deeper qualities, such as shared values, how they treated their family or their potential as a parent.

Similarly, in my professional journey, my job choices were often driven by salary, status, or job title. I seldom delved into deeper, reflective questions such as:

- Would I genuinely enjoy collaborating with my colleagues, and does the workplace culture foster personal growth?
- Does my supervisor embody the qualities of a supportive leader or exhibit toxic managerial tendencies?
- Does the work I'm pursuing align harmoniously with my core values and principles?

When I got specific with what I sought by intentionally identifying what I desired with precision and deliberation, I found my soulmate and true calling and purpose.

I didn't realize it then, but I was aimlessly going through life without a clear destination and wondering why I kept repeating the same mistakes.

The underlying lesson is this: clarity is paramount when defining your desires, be it in relationships, friendships, or career choices. You need to be specific with what you want in life.

What do you want from a partner, friendship, or career? It is essential to resist the temptation to let external pressures dictate these choices, be it societal expectations or the desires of others.

Instead, ask yourself, "What do I genuinely want from life?" Be specific, be clear, and be unwavering in your intentionality.

The lesson is clear: unwavering clarity regarding your life aspirations and professional journey is imperative. Otherwise, others may fill that void with their expectations and desires.

💡 Exercise: Clarify Your Life and Career Desires

This exercise aims to help you gain clarity on your life and career aspirations by reflecting on the lessons presented in the passage. By answering a series of questions, you'll uncover your core values, preferences, and desires, ultimately guiding you toward making more informed decisions in your personal and professional life.

Self-Reflection on Life Goals:

a. Take a few minutes to ponder your life goals and what truly matters to you. Consider what you want to achieve in your personal life, relationships, and overall happiness.
b. Write down your answers to the following questions:

- What are your top three life priorities or values?
- What qualities or characteristics are essential in your ideal life partner or close relationships?
- What aspects of your life contribute most to your sense of purpose and fulfillment?

Self-Reflection on Career Goals:

a. Shift your focus to your career aspirations. Think about your current or future career path and what you want to achieve professionally.

b. Write down your answers to the following questions:

- Beyond salary and job title, what are the most critical factors in your ideal job or career?
- What kind of work environment or culture do you thrive in, and what motivates you?
- How does your current or desired career align with your core values and principles?

Identify Areas of Alignment:

a. Review your responses to both questions (life and career goals).
b. Identify common themes, values, or desires that emerge in your personal and professional aspirations.
c. Consider how aligning your values with your career choices can contribute to a more fulfilling life.

Set Actionable Goals:

a. Based on your reflections and areas of alignment, set at least one actionable goal for your personal life and one for your career.
b. These goals should be specific, measurable, achievable, relevant, and time-bound (SMART).

Create a Plan:

a. Develop a brief action plan for each goal, outlining the steps you need to take to work toward achieving them.
b. Consider potential obstacles and how you can overcome them.
c. Set deadlines or milestones to track your progress.

Regularly Review and Adjust:

a. Commit to periodically reviewing your goals and action plans to ensure they remain aligned with your evolving desires and values. Adjust as necessary to continue toward a more purposeful life and fulfilling career.

Remember that gaining clarity and aligning your goals with your values is ongoing. By consistently reflecting on your desires and taking intentional steps, you can work towards achieving a more meaningful and satisfying life.

PURSUE YOUR JOY

"Be fearless in the pursuit of what sets your soul on fire."
—Jennifer Lee

Don't wait for perfection.
Bet on yourself.
Don't wait for someone to choose you.
Bet on yourself.
Don't wait for the right time.
The right time has always been now.

What sets your soul on fire?
Do more of that.
What brings you joy?
Do more of that.
What brings you peace?
Do more of that.
What brings you health?
Do more of that?
What brings you, love?
Do more of that.

The simple act of believing in yourself is powerful. All significant change happens when you think "it is possible."

💡 Exercise: What Sets Your Soul on Fire

This exercise aims to rekindle your passions and prioritize activities that bring you profound joy and fulfillment. You can infuse your life with enthusiasm and purpose by identifying ten things that set your soul on fire and scheduling one of them immediately.

Take a moment to reflect on activities, interests, or experiences that genuinely ignite your passion. These could be hobbies, creative pursuits, adventures, or anything that fills you with joy. Create a list of ten things that set your soul on fire. Write them down in your journal or on a digital note.

Review your list and immediately select one passion or activity you're eager to pursue. Consider the feasibility of scheduling this activity in your calendar today or within the next few days.

Open your calendar, whether it's digital or physical. Allocate a specific time slot for the chosen passion or activity. Be precise about when and for how long you will engage in it. Treat this scheduled time as non-negotiable, just like you would for work meetings or other commitments.

Follow through with your scheduled passion or activity session. Whether it's dancing, trying a new restaurant, practicing a craft, or pursuing any other passion, make it a priority. Fully immerse yourself in the experience and savor every moment.

After completing your chosen passion activity, take some time to reflect on how it made you feel and the impact it had on your overall well-being. Consider scheduling another passion session soon and repeat this exercise regularly to keep the flame of your passions burning brightly.

Remember, prioritizing activities that bring you joy, and fulfillment is essential for your happiness. By scheduling and committing to these passions, you're taking proactive steps to nurture your well-being and create a balanced, fulfilling life.

"Love the person you are today but fight like hell to become the person you aspire to be tomorrow."

–Lan Phan

Life is not all or nothing. It's complex and nuanced. You can simultaneously strive for self-improvement while appreciating the person you are today. Balancing both realms paves the way to contentment and personal growth.

Set realistic expectations but work hard at surpassing them.

Stop hating yourself and punishing yourself for not being where you want to be. Stop moving the finish line every time you reach a goal.

Learn to pause and celebrate the progress you worked hard for, but don't be satisfied with the status quo.

As you continue your journey forward, do so with an unwavering appreciation for your present growth and the milestones you've achieved.

In short, have gratitude for who you are today, but fight like hell to become the person you aspire to be tomorrow.

CELEBRATE YOUR PROGRESS

"I'm not where I want to be, but I'm proud that I'm not where I used to be."
—Joyce Meyer.

It's okay to want more. But we must pause and appreciate how far we've gone. Yeah, I'm looking at you.

Life is not just about arriving at your destination. It's about the journey and who you become along the way. Cherish the distance you've traveled.

You worked hard.
Pause.
Celebrate.
And if you see someone else working hard and progressing, celebrate their journey, too.
Clap for your friends.

💡 **Exercise: Identify five milestones you've reached in the last five years. Celebrate these milestones and reflect on what you've learned in the process.**

"Stop comparing yourself to others. The only person you should be competing against is the reflection you see in the mirror. Your one goal in life: to be a better person than you were yesterday."

–Lan Phan

STOP COMPARING YOURSELF TO OTHERS

Other people are not your competition. Your only competition is the person looking back at you in the mirror. Comparing yourself with others only distracts you from your goals. Focus on being a better person than yesterday.

Maintain a laser focus on your personal goals.

Ask yourself these questions:

What is your purpose?
Why is it important to you?
What is your art?
Are you focused on creating the best possible you?
What are you doing daily to become the best version of yourself?

Author Seth Godin discusses the importance of discovering and sharing our art with the world. Everyone's canvas is distinct, and their experiences are uniquely their own.

Remember, no one can be you. To unearth your purpose, turn inward and reflect. We must quiet the noise of the world that demands that we conform to a one-size-fits-all definition of success.

YOUR MINDSET CREATES YOUR DESTINY

Change Your Mindset, Change Your Life

Your Mindset Creates Your Future

Your mindset serves as the blueprint for your future, defining the lens through which you view the world and molding your beliefs, attitudes, and mental frameworks. It shapes how you perceive yourself and directs your daily choices and actions.

Imagine your mindset as the operating system for your brain, functioning like software that governs your thoughts, emotions, and responses in various situations. Just as you have different apps on your phone for different tasks, your mindset determines your approach to life's challenges and opportunities.

Our mindset reflects our worldview and life philosophy, often sculpted by the shared values of our social and cultural environment. It's more than a mere collection of thoughts; it forms the foundation of our beliefs, shaping how we perceive the world and our role within it, ultimately influencing our thoughts, emotions, and behaviors.

In essence, our mindset and thoughts define our identity. To transform your life, you must initiate a shift in your mindset. As Albert Einstein famously said, 'The definition of insanity is doing the same thing over and over again and expecting a different result." The same principle applies to our mindset—expecting different outcomes necessitates changing how we think and perceive the world.

If you desire change, you must change your mindset. Your mindset serves as the craftsman of your self-construction, molding your life attitudes, choices, and even your approach to collaboration versus competition.

Ultimately, your mindset exerts a profound influence on your reality, echoing the wisdom of Henry Ford: 'Whether you think you can, or you think you can't, you're right.'

Fixed vs. Growth Mindset

In her book 'Mindset: The New Psychology of Success,' Stanford behavioral psychologist Carol Dweck identifies two primary mindsets: fixed and growth mindsets. A fixed mindset believes in static abilities and inherent talent, while a growth mindset sees potential for growth and development through effort and perseverance.

As the name implies, individuals with fixed mindsets believe their abilities are fixed and static, believing people are inherently talented and intelligent. In contrast, those with a growth mindset view talent and intelligence as qualities that can be nurtured through hard work and unwavering perseverance. They believe that everyone can get better with effort and hard work.

Studies have shown that your mindset profoundly influences how you navigate life's challenges. For instance, those with a growth mindset exhibit an appetite for learning and a relentless work ethic, understanding that these efforts translate into a more enriched life and personal advancement. Conversely, those with a fixed mindset may shy away from pursuits, convinced they lack natural ability. For instance, a student who asserts, "I'm not good at math, so I can't become an engineer."

In addition, individuals with a growth mindset are less inclined to surrender when confronted with adversity; they view failure as an opportunity for learning and personal growth. In contrast, someone with a fixed mindset may be more prone to give up, believing they lack the capacity for improvement.

Living a purpose-driven life requires a growth mindset, making it an essential prerequisite for personal growth.

Each of Us Possesses the Capacity to Cultivate a Growth Mindset

The good news is that everyone can nurture a growth mindset. In the forthcoming pages, we will offer techniques to surmount negative emotions and cultivate the mindset necessary to fulfill your purpose.

We can't change our past, but it is within the power of each of us to initiate transformative changes in our lives. It is never too late to embark on the journey of personal growth and become the person you were always destined to be. However, this endeavor requires dedication, time, and a steadfast belief in your potential for change and growth.

Remember that you have the potential to change your life at any moment. Your voyage toward growth is already underway. You took the first step by reading this book. Now, all you need is to keep going toward the path of your dreams and aspirations.

How Your Mindset Activates Your Reticular Activating System

If you want to understand the science behind how your mindset shapes your brain's function and, consequently, your future, read on. If not, skip to the next section. This knowledge is crucial as it sheds light on our mindset's profound impact on our internal development.

In our ancestral past, the Reticular Activating System (RAS) played a pivotal role in survival. It rapidly alerted us to potential dangers, such as saber-toothed tigers, while guiding us towards essentials like food and water. Think of your RAS as your brain's built-in security system, designed to protect you from harm and focus on vital survival needs.

Your RAS acts as your brain's attention director, constantly sifting through sensory input to determine relevance. It functions as a gatekeeper, filtering important information from the vast sea of sensory data. Moreover, your RAS serves as a personal assistant for your goals. Setting a goal or having a strong desire helps your brain notice relevant opportunities, serving as a built-in reminder system.

Your mindset actively communicates with your RAS, instructing it on what to prioritize as important or unimportant. Essentially, we are the architects of our destiny. When you seek personal growth and development, your brain acts as a filter, homing in on precisely what you seek amid life's noise. Conversely, a fixed mindset, believing in incapacity for learning and growth, becomes a self-fulfilling prophecy.

In simpler terms, think of the Reticular Activating System as your brain's attention manager. It decides what warrants attention, keeps you alert when necessary, and aids in focusing on your goals. It functions like a spotlight, illuminating what matters most to you in your world.

To summarize, your mindset shapes the activation of your RAS by directing your cognitive focus, establishing goals and intentions, and creating emotional connections with specific ideas or objectives. Consequently, your RAS filters and prioritizes information in alignment with your mindset, facilitating the recognition of opportunities and experiences consistent with your beliefs and goals.

This interplay between mindset and the RAS significantly influences your perception of the world and your capacity to achieve desired outcomes.

Unleashing the Power of Belief: How Your Thoughts Shape Your Reality

So how can you actively nurture a positive mindset?

If you've already engaged in the exercises from Lesson 1, you've taken the initial step toward cultivating a more positive mindset by pinpointing your true purpose.

When you possess a well-defined purpose and unwavering core values, your brain via your reticular activating system (RAS)—the neural component responsible for prioritizing information deserving of your attention while dismissing the irrelevant—functions as a filter, effectively sieving out distractions and sharpening your focus on the elements that drive you toward your goals and passions. Your RAS, coupled with intention and purpose, becomes a guiding beacon, shedding light on what truly matters in your life.

Now that your mind is finely tuned to your purpose, the subsequent step entails embracing the belief that you (yes, you!) can embark on a transformative journey, evolving into someone who lives their purpose. Spoiler alert: this metamorphosis hinges on cultivating a growth mindset.

"If our thoughts are the architects of our reality, let us cultivate thoughts of prosperity, health, abundance, joy, love, and serenity.

Rather than dwelling on thoughts of fear, let us focus on our aspirations. Let us focus on hope. Let us draw strength from our faith."

–Lan Phan

TREASURE YOUR VALLEYS

When you're going through difficulties, envisioning the end of the struggle is often challenging.

But what if the difficulties are not obstacles but the prerequisites for your next adventure? What if they are chiseling you into the person you need to become to achieve your dreams?

Know this: there is light at the end of the tunnel. Keep moving forward, one step at a time.

If uncertainty clouds your path, focus on doing the next right thing and then the next right thing after that. Keep on going until you get clarity.

Success isn't a straight path; it's an intricate journey with a winding roadmap.

Remind yourself that mountains cannot exist without the valleys.

Growth occurs when you embrace the valleys with the same enthusiasm as the peaks.

YOUR THOUGHTS SHAPE YOUR FUTURE

*"If you realized how powerful your thoughts are, you
would never think a negative thought."*
—Peace Pilgrim

On an average day, our minds churn out approximately 60,000 thoughts. Remarkably, many of these thoughts tend to be repetitive, playing like a broken record throughout our lifetimes. What is the story your thoughts are telling you?

Why do you let negative thoughts like fear, anger, and jealousy into your life? Such emotions should never be greeted as welcome guests. This doesn't mean we should suppress our negative emotions.

We must respect all of our feelings. Even our most painful ones are harbingers intended to protect us from harm, and some help drive us to excel. However, when these negative emotions become debilitating, we must strengthen our resolve to counter them with an unshakable belief in ourselves.

Be mindful of your thoughts, but mindfulness doesn't equal suppressing negative emotions. Quite the opposite, it means acknowledging and respecting your feelings.

Sometimes, these emotions serve as signposts, directing you inward to address areas needing healing. At other times, they guide you away from harmful situations or individuals. Occasionally, they propel you to pursue what you once deemed impossible. When harnessed, negative emotions can serve as catalysts for positive change.

While it's essential to honor your feelings, it's equally vital not to dwell on negative emotions. Think of these emotions as tunnels. You should navigate through them, but never reside within them too long. Always move toward the light. Over time, lingering negative emotions can inflict physical and mental harm.

💡 Exercise: Transforming Your Self-Talk for Positive Empowerment

Today, take a moment to reflect on your inner dialogue. Did you catch yourself uttering any self-critical or negative thoughts about yourself? If so, jot down those negative comments.

Now, let's embark on the empowering journey of reframing these thoughts into positive, uplifting messages. For example, if you find yourself thinking, "I'm too old," consider transforming it into a powerful affirmation like, "I've gained invaluable wisdom through my life experiences, and each passing year brings me closer to becoming the person I am meant to be."

Challenge yourself to reframe at least one negative thought into a positive, empowering statement. This exercise can be a small step toward reshaping your thought patterns and, ultimately, your mindset for a brighter, more optimistic future.

Nothing in the World Happens *to* You. It Happens *for* You

This is a hard lesson to grasp, but when we begin to understand this life lesson, our perspective broadens, and genuine personal growth can happen.

While many aspects of life remain beyond our control, we can shape how we interpret and react to those situations.

Every experience can be viewed as a gift or a curse. We have the autonomy to select whether we play the role of the victim or the hero in our narrative.

The choice is entirely our own.

Choose to see the experience as a valuable gift. Consider it a lesson that propels you forward into the next chapter of your journey. Choose to be the hero of your narrative.

By mastering our emotions and crafting the stories we tell ourselves, we can script our life journeys and shape our destinies.

Don't allow others to dictate your narrative; seize the pen and author your compelling story.

💡 Exercise: Transforming Challenges into Growth

Think about a difficulty or challenge you've encountered in your life. It could be a personal, professional, or emotional obstacle. Reflect on the positive outcomes that emerged from this experience. What valuable lessons did you learn? How did this challenge ultimately pave the way for something even better in your life?

For example, I left San Francisco years ago after a painful breakup and relocated to New York. I was heartbroken at the time. However, a few months after the move, I had the opportunity to meet my future husband. Today, we've been happily married for over a decade.

Share how your darkest days can lead to beautiful and unexpected outcomes. This exercise invites you to recognize the growth and transformation that can arise from challenges, reminding us that sometimes, our struggles become the catalysts for our most remarkable life chapters.

"Pay close attention to your inner dialogue, for it possesses the extraordinary power to shape your destiny, serving either as a constructive force or a formidable obstacle."

–Lan Phan

TRANSFORMING YOUR INNER DIALOGUE

Reframing your mental dialogue can be transformative – helping reshape your life's course. Sometimes, the slightest shifts in your vocabulary can yield profound changes in your life's direction. Consider the addition of a single word: "yet."

"I can't do this" becomes "I can't do this yet."
"I don't understand" transforms into "I don't understand yet."

This simple addition is a valuable tool for cultivating a growth mindset. It signifies the acknowledgment that progress takes effort. It's a gentle reminder that learning is a journey, not an instant result, helping you transition from a fixed mindset to one that thrives on growth.

You can edit your self-talk in various ways:
Instead of saying, "I don't know," declare, "I will learn how."
Rather than asking, "Why do I have to do this," affirm, "I get to do this."

Shift from asking, "Why is this happening to me?" to the empowering inquiry, "Why is this happening for me?"

Remember, external events shape a mere 20 percent of your life, but the remaining eighty percent is influenced by your mental constructs and how you interpret those events. Let that sink in.

Harness the incredible potential of your inner dialogue, and you can transform your life overnight.

Identify three things that pique your curiosity areas you currently lack knowledge in but yearn to explore. Write them down and then add the powerful word "yet" to each sentence. For example:

"I don't know how to start a company ... yet."

This exercise serves as a reminder of the potential for growth and learning within you. Your choice of words shapes your mindset, and by embracing the word "yet," you acknowledge that your journey is a path of continuous development and expansion. Your words are the seeds of your future, so choose them wisely.

💡 Exercise: Transforming Challenges to Growth Opportunities

Take a moment to reflect on a challenging situation you are currently navigating. Rather than asking yourself, "Why is this happening to me?" consider reframing the question as, "What is this trying to teach me?"

Now, write about this challenging situation and explore the lessons it might offer you. How could this experience propel you forward, shape your growth, or guide you toward the next phase of your journey?

This exercise encourages you to embrace difficulties as opportunities for personal development and self-discovery, offering a fresh perspective that can illuminate the hidden wisdom within life's challenges.

EMBRACE THE COURAGE TO FAIL

*"Do not judge me by my successes. Judge me by how
many times I fell down and got back up again."*
—Nelson Mandela

Don't fear failure. Fear the prospect of not living the life you dream of due to that fear. The only way you can indeed fail is by never attempting at all.

In any new venture's early stages, struggling and stumbling is to be expected. You may find yourself far from proficient, and that's perfectly fine. Release the pressure and enjoy the process, whether you're learning a new language, dancing, or embarking on a new business venture.

To quote John Acuff, "Be brave enough to suck at something new."

Just as we wouldn't blame a toddler for faltering while learning to walk, we should be equally forgiving and compassionate toward ourselves. Every instance of rising after a fall fortifies our inner strength and determination.

When you fall, get right back up. Just don't quit. Keep going. Refuse to surrender and remember that progress is born from persistence. Remember, it's always hard before you get good.

💡 Exercise: Confront Your Fears and Embrace Growth

Challenge yourself right now to engage in an activity that triggers fear or discomfort. It could be initiating a conversation with a stranger, reaching out to a friend, expressing admiration for someone's smile, taking on a challenging project, or addressing public speaking.

The only way to get better at anything is to do it until it gets less scary. Your body can't tell the difference between fear and excitement. So, tell yourself you're excited.

This exercise encourages you to step out of your comfort zone, seize opportunities for personal growth, and discover that what once appeared daunting can become an exhilarating source of self-improvement and empowerment.

REJECTION IS REDIRECTION

"Rejection is merely a redirection; A course correction to your destiny."
—Bryant McGill

Sometimes, you can only get clarity when looking in the rear-view mirror.

Rejection, undeniably, can be a painful experience. However, it's crucial to recognize that rejection often serves as a guiding force, redirecting us toward the paths we are truly destined to traverse.

Rejection has often served as a redirection and a path to new beginnings. Many times, these were beautiful new beginnings I would not have voluntarily taken otherwise.

Rejection is akin to divine protection, shielding us from what is not meant for us. Looking back, I can pinpoint moments when opportunities seemed to slip through my fingers, only to realize that they were guiding lights illuminating the way to my true purpose.

Several years ago, a promotion and pay raise offered and then rescinded due to my pregnancy ultimately propelled me to leave a toxic work environment I had endured for far too long.

When I faced job loss at the onset of the COVID-19 pandemic, I initially mourned losing what I thought was my dream job. Little did I know that this adversity would serve as the catalyst for creating "Community of Seven," my dream company.

Closed doors, in reality, often lead us to opportunities and blessings far beyond what we could have ever imagined. And sometimes, they safeguard us from journeys not aligned with our true calling.

For those currently grappling with job loss or facing other significant challenges, it's essential to remember that what's for you cannot be taken away—a destiny greater and more fulfilling than you can envision awaits you.

💡 Exercise: Embracing Rejection as Your Redirection

Take a moment to reflect on a significant rejection or setback you've encountered in your life. It could be a missed opportunity, a denied aspiration, or a challenging situation that led to a sense of rejection.

Now, in writing, explore how that rejection eventually redirected you towards a more promising path or a new opportunity. Consider how it protected you from a journey not meant for you or helped you make a crucial course correction.

As you do this exercise, you'll gain insights into how rejection has played a transformative role in your journey, reinforcing that sometimes, closed doors lead to unexpected blessings and guide you toward your true destiny.

Kintsugi

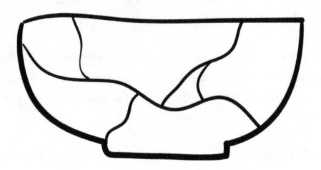

"You Are Not Broken.

Your cracks and crevices, trials and tribulations, and rejections have shaped the person you are today.

In a society that praises perfection, be the person who embraces flaws, scars, and imperfections. They are not evidence of weakness but proof that you have lived and are stronger than what tried to hurt you."

–Lan Phan

YOU ARE NOT BROKEN

Your cracks and crevices, trials and tribulations, and rejections have shaped the person you are today.

Kintsugi is the Japanese artistry of mending broken pottery with gold lacquer. It is built on the idea that we can create something more exquisite and resilient by embracing our flaws and imperfections.

Instead of repairing the pottery like new, each fracture and gap is not concealed but enriched with precious gold. Every break becomes a one-of-a-kind masterpiece. Rather than restoring the item to its original state, artisans celebrate the "scars" as an integral part of the design.

In many ways, the mended pottery is a metaphor for our healing journey. It imparts valuable lessons: sometimes, in repairing what is broken, we create something more beautiful, substantial, and uniquely our own.

Whether you're navigating the loss of a job or a loved one or facing personal adversity, remember that emerging from these trials can forge a newfound strength. Remember, scar tissue has always been stronger than healthy skin.

You won't realize your full potential until you endure challenging times. Growth occurs on the other side of the challenge. Remember that.

Lastly, in a society that praises perfection, be the person who embraces flaws, scars, and imperfections. They are not evidence of weakness but proof that you have lived and are stronger than what tried to hurt you.

💡 Exercise: Embracing Your Personal Kintsugi Journey

Reflect on a challenging experience that left you feeling broken or scarred in some way. It could be a rejection, a setback, a loss, or any significant trial you've faced.

Now, imagine yourself as a Kintsugi artisan, mending the broken pieces of your experience with seams of gold. In writing, describe how you would embrace and celebrate the flaws and imperfections that this experience brought into your life. What unique beauty and strength do these "scars" contribute to your story and identity?

Consider the idea that, like the mended pottery, your journey of healing and growth has made you more beautiful, resilient, and unique. Share how you can see your journey as a work of art, highlighting the valuable lessons and strengths that have emerged from your challenges.

This exercise encourages you to reframe your perspective on past difficulties, seeing them not as sources of weakness but as integral parts of your unique and beautiful journey.

"Stop waiting for someone to save you.

You have always been the hero in your story."

–Lan Phan

STOP WAITING TO BE SAVED

Your life undergoes a remarkable transformation when you choose to cast aside self-doubt, venture beyond your comfort zone, and embark on a voyage of personal and professional advancement.

The road to success is closely tied to your unwavering dedication to daily, steadfast personal and professional growth.

Success isn't an arbitrary stroke of luck; it's something you actively create by becoming the best version of yourself.

If you want change, remember that it always begins with you.

Stop waiting for someone to save you. You have always been the hero in your story.

EMBRACE THE POWER OF THE PRESENT MOMENT

"Make the most of today. Don't allow the troubles
of yesterday to steal the gift of right now"
—Kristen Butler

Take a deep, conscious breath.
Pause and be genuinely grateful for this moment.

The past, laden with regrets, and the future, tinged with fears, are but mental constructs. The only thing real is this exact moment—the now. Within this moment, all that truly matters is that you are alive—the air filling your lungs is a testament to your connection to the universe and all that surrounds you.

But why is being present so important?

Clarity and Awareness: When you reside in the present, your mind becomes clearer, and your awareness sharpens. You can better perceive the beauty, nuances, and opportunities surrounding you.

Reducing Stress and Anxiety: Anxiety often arises from fretting about the future or ruminating on the past. You can alleviate stress and find tranquility by grounding yourself in the present.

Authentic Connections: Being fully present when interacting with others fosters more profound, authentic connections. It shows respect, empathy, and genuine interest.

Maximizing Productivity: Concentrating on the task at hand, free from distractions from past regrets or future worries, enhances efficiency and productivity.

Emotional Balance: The present moment is a sanctuary where you can manage your emotions better. It enables you to respond to situations more rationally and thoughtfully.

So, as you breathe and express gratitude for this moment, remember that life unfolds in the present. Embrace it with openness and mindfulness, for within it lies the key to a more prosperous, fulfilling existence.

💡 Exercise: Staying in the Present Moment

In our fast-paced lives, it's easy to get caught up in the rush of daily routines and the pull of past regrets or future worries. This exercise aims to help you cultivate a deeper appreciation for the present moment.

Mindful Breathing: Find a quiet, comfortable space where you won't be disturbed. Set a timer for 5 minutes. Close your eyes, take a few deep breaths, and then allow your breath to return to its natural rhythm. Focus all your attention on the sensation of your breath entering and leaving your body. If your mind wanders, gently bring your focus back to your breath.

Sensory Exploration: Step outside or sit by a window where you can see nature. Engage your senses fully for 10 minutes. What do you see, hear, smell, taste, and touch? Take in the details of your surroundings with curiosity and appreciation.

Technology-Free Meal: During your next meal, put away all electronic devices. Instead, savor each bite mindfully. Pay attention to the textures, flavors, and aromas of your food. Eat slowly and deliberately, without rushing.

Gratitude Journal: Start a gratitude journal. Every day, write down three things you're grateful for in the present moment. These can be simple pleasures or meaningful experiences.

Mindful Conversation: Engage in a conversation with someone, whether a friend, a family member, or a colleague. Practice active listening by giving them your full attention. Avoid the urge to interrupt or think about what you'll say next. Be present in the exchange.

Daily Reflection: At the end of the day, take a few minutes to reflect on your experiences. What moments today brought you joy, peace, or a sense of fulfillment? Write them down in a journal.

This exercise encourages you to make the present moment a conscious part of your daily life. Regularly engaging in these practices will sharpen your awareness and deepen your appreciation for the richness of each moment. Over time, your overall sense of well-being and contentment increases as you embrace the gift of the present.

STOP BURNOUT IN ITS TRACKS

Signs you may be heading towards burnout:

- Neglecting Your Own Needs
- Weak Boundaries
- Overextending Yourself
- Prioritizing Others Over Yourself
- Consistently Neglecting Self-Care
- Excessive Workload
- Unhealthy Dietary Choices
- Sedentary Lifestyle
- Isolation
- Lack of Purpose
- Dependence on Stimulants
- Ignoring Digestive Health
- Unrelenting, Chronic Stress

Did you read this list and think, "That sounds like me"? If these signs hit close to home, you might be on the path to burnout or already be going through it. This way of life can be detrimental to your well-being and requires addressing.

Here's the reality: Burnout doesn't magically disappear. You must take action to change your environment or reassess your lifestyle.

If you find yourself caught in these behaviors, consider the following steps:

- Seek Support: Don't hesitate to ask for help from friends, family, or professionals.
- Set Boundaries: Establish clear boundaries in your personal and work life to protect your mental and emotional well-being.
- Prioritize Mental and Physical Health: Invest in self-care practices, including adequate rest and sleep, to replenish your well-being.
- Take Breaks: Schedule regular breaks in your daily routine to recharge and regain focus.

- Professional Help: Consult a mental health professional to navigate these challenging emotions if needed.

Learn from my mistakes. I've faced burnout multiple times in my life and only emerged from those dark periods when I took one or more of these actions:

- Seek Help: Reaching out for support from those around me.
- Leave Negative Environments: Exiting situations that were detrimental to my well-being.
- Change Behaviors: Altering my actions and choices.

As we approach the brink, especially amid the complexities of caregiving, economic uncertainty, stress, and demanding work environments, we must step back and evaluate why we feel this way. More importantly, we must identify the actions needed to address burnout.

These negative emotions are like a tunnel—you must navigate through them toward the light. They don't simply vanish by wishing them away. If you want change, you must be willing to change.

💡 Exercise: Addressing Burnout

If you're grappling with burnout, you must analyze your current situation and pinpoint the underlying causes. Follow these steps to address and mitigate burnout:

Identify Burnout Triggers: Look closely at your daily life and work. What specific factors are contributing to your burnout? Recognize the areas where you feel overwhelmed or stretched thin.

Embrace the Power of "No": If you constantly say yes to too many commitments, it's time to learn the art of saying no. Understand that saying no is not a sign of weakness; it's a means of preserving your well-being.

Seek Support: If saying no isn't an option due to work or personal obligations, consider requesting help or additional assistance from your colleagues, friends, or family. Delegate tasks or share responsibilities to ease the load.

Prioritize Self-Care: Make self-care a non-negotiable priority. Allocate time for activities that replenish your mental and emotional resources. Whether exercising, relaxing, doing hobbies, or spending time with loved ones, ensure self-care is part of your routine.

Reduce Exposure to Stressors: Identify the stressors in your life, both at work and in your personal life. Determine ways to minimize exposure to these stressors. This may involve setting boundaries, seeking solutions, or reevaluating commitments.

Optimize Time Off: If you have paid time off (PTO) available, use it wisely. Feel free to take breaks when needed. During these pauses, disconnect from work-related matters and focus on rejuvenating yourself.

Remember, addressing burnout is a process that requires self-awareness and proactive steps. By identifying the root causes and taking action to protect your well-being, you can regain balance and resilience in your life.

YOU
ARE ENOUGH.

Stop measuring your life against the idealized portrayals of people you see in magazines and television.

End the ceaseless comparison to airbrushed and fabricated images on social media.

No, you don't need to lose 10 more pounds, but it's crucial to rid the weight of doubt, guilt, and insecurities. Release the weight of other people's expectations. That's the real burden that's been holding you down.

In a world that perpetually implies you're inadequate, all in the pursuit of selling you things that only enrich someone else, allow me to be the voice that asserts:

YOU ARE ENOUGH.

Actually, I think you're pretty amazing. So stop comparing yourself to people you don't even know.

Let go of the doubt.

And focus on becoming the best version of yourself.

Embrace your unique journey.

IT'S OK NOT TO BE OK

"Sometimes the best salve is to simply be ok with not being ok.
No one is ok all the time, even though we like to pretend so."
—Unknown

Stop pretending that everything is okay. We often bury our emotions or try to numb them with various coping mechanisms, such as food, alcohol, or distractions, hoping they'll magically disappear. However, it's essential to acknowledge that negative emotions are a natural part of life.

Stress, worry, regret, and fear all serve a vital purpose: they are our body's warning signals when something is amiss. They exist to protect us from both real and perceived dangers. Sometimes, negative emotions guide us to discover what we truly desire in life. After all, how can we appreciate happiness and love without understanding pain and heartache? However, it's vital to view negative emotions like a tunnel. We must go through them but never linger in the darkness. We must always move toward the light.

So, practice self-compassion. Allow yourself to experience these emotions without judgment. Sit with them, but do not allow them to overwhelm you. Create some distance between yourself and the emotion, recognizing that they are feelings and do not define your identity. These emotions are temporary visitors, delivering messages that can guide you. When you master and navigate these emotions, you gain mastery over your life.

💡 Exercise: Take a Moment to Reflect on Your Current Emotional State

Take a moment to think about a recent negative emotion or feeling you've experienced. It could be stress, anxiety, sadness, anger, or any other emotion. As you recall this emotion, remember that it's a natural part of being human. Practice self-compassion by acknowledging that it's okay to feel this way. Use phrases like "I am allowed to feel this emotion, but the emotions do not define me."

LAN PHAN

Imagine your feelings as artifacts, separate from your identity. You can give your emotion a name. For example, acknowledging it as "anxiety." Naming the emotion can help you separate it from your identity.

Using the tunnel analogy, visualize a tunnel. Imagine this negative emotion as a tunnel. You are entering this tunnel, and there is a bright light at the other end. Mentally, step into the tunnel and know that you are moving through this emotion, not avoiding it. Pay attention to any insights or lessons this emotion is trying to convey. Is there something it's urging you to address or change in your life? As you progress through the tunnel, focus on the light at the end. This represents moving beyond the negative emotion and towards a place of clarity, peace, and personal growth. When you're ready, visualize yourself emerging from the tunnel, leaving the negative emotion behind.

This exercise aims to help you develop a healthier relationship with your emotions, acknowledging them as messengers rather than obstacles. Embrace the negative emotions as part of your human experience, and practice letting go when they have served their purpose.

NEVER UNDERESTIMATE HOW STRONG YOU ARE

"When the roots are deep, there is no reason to fear the wind."
—African Proverb

Do not underestimate the depth of your strength.
Your roots run deep, intertwining with the earth, rock, and water. You are the living embodiment of the indomitable spirits of your ancestors, who endured the harshest trials of war, famine, and untold hardships.

You were born from their unbreakable strength and resilience.

The simple fact of your existence is a testament that you have overcome every challenge that sought to inflict harm upon you. You have weathered the storm and prevailed.

Never, ever underestimate the extraordinary strength that resides within you. Your very presence attests to your unwavering triumph over the trials of your past.

💡 Exercise: Close Your Eyes and Engage in Mindful Breathing

Visualize yourself as a towering, majestic Oak tree radiating strength and pride. Feel your roots extending deeply into the earth, connecting you to your ancestors, your unwavering strength, resilience, legacy, and faith. These are the unshakable anchors that firmly secure you to the ground. Embrace the knowledge that you need not fear any approaching storm, for your roots run deep, providing unwavering stability.

APPRECIATING YOUR SCARS

*"Sometimes you get what you want. Other times, you get a lesson
in patience, timing, alignment, empathy, compassion, faith,
perseverance, resilience, humility, trust, meaning, awareness, resistance,
purpose, clarity, grief, beauty, and life. Either way, you win."*
—Brianne Wiest

You won't always get what you want; sometimes, that's the best thing to happen to you. Thank goodness we didn't get half the things we thought we wanted when we were younger.

If we got everything we wanted handed to us on a silver plate—how could we cultivate the qualities of resilience, determination, and humility? Just as our muscles grow stronger through the small tears they endure during exercise, we also strengthen our inner selves through the trials, disappointments, and heartaches we overcome.

Your unique beauty radiates from the scars that mark you, each mark telling a story only you can share. Embrace those scars and imperfections, for they've played an integral part in shaping the person you've become at this very moment.

Let me leave you with this transformative quote from Rumi: "The wound is the place where the light enters you." Often, our pain and hardship allow our inner light and spirit to shine brightly.

💡 **Exercise:** Reflect on a moment when something you desired wasn't granted, but it was a hidden blessing. What insights did you gain from that situation? Take time to jot down the valuable lessons you learned from this experience.

EMBRACE UNCERTAINTY

"Trust the Wait. Embrace the uncertainty. Enjoy the beauty of becoming. When nothing is certain, anything is possible."
—Mandy Hale

Change can feel scary, yet it also carries the potential for profound growth if we open ourselves to it. It's a force that can propel you towards your dreams and aspirations if you allow it into your life.

Approach change with an open heart and a curious mind. Although it may initially appear daunting, acquiring new experiences and opportunities, holds the potential for untold rewards and personal development.

Consider change as a potent catalyst for positive transformation. Inviting it into your life opens doors to unexpected blessings and unforeseen outcomes. As you navigate the ever-shifting tides of change, maintain a hopeful perspective and witness how it unfolds, enriching and expanding the dimensions of your life's journey.

💡 **Exercise: Reflect on a recent change or transition, whether a shift in your routine, a new job, or a personal development journey.**

Write down how this change has influenced your life positively. How has it contributed to your growth and development? Emphasize the blessings that emerged from this change. How did you grow and develop because of it?

Think about a current change or challenge you are facing or anticipate facing soon. Write down your initial feelings and thoughts about it. How might you approach this challenge with an open heart and a curious mind? What potential rewards or personal development opportunities might it hold?

Remember that change is an inevitable part of life, and your ability to embrace it with optimism and an open heart can lead to remarkable personal growth and enrich your life journey.

BE HELPFUL

"Great leaders know they're not the smartest person in the room."
—Gifford Thomas

One of the most valuable pieces of advice came from a Stanford University professor, who told me, "Lan, you'll achieve much more in life if you aim to be the most helpful person in the room rather than the smartest."

As a leader, your goal shouldn't be to be the most intelligent person in the room. Instead, you should aspire to surround yourself with the best talent.

Avoid micromanagement and view your team as valuable assets driving the organization forward, not as threats to your position. Actively cultivate the next generation of leaders, providing them with the training and resources they need to succeed.

In this role, see yourself as their guide and supporter.

Genuine leaders are self-assured in their skills and actively foster the growth of those around them. You can only be a truly effective leader once you start nurturing more leaders. Read that once again.

🔦 Exercise: Reflect on the individuals you admire most and who have impacted you significantly.

What specific qualities or characteristics about them stand out to you and make you appreciate their presence in your life? Write this in your journal.

DO WHAT'S RIGHT FOR *YOU*

"You can lie down for people to walk on you, and they will
still complain that you're not flat enough. Live your life."
—Ritu Ghatourey

Stop letting people walk over you.

Recognize that not everyone will find joy in your happiness. Stop giving them the power to ruin your day. What they think of you is none of your business.

Do what's right for yourself instead of letting others dictate your mood. Establish boundaries and develop the strength to stand up for yourself. Remember that safeguarding your happiness and well-being is paramount.

Instead of those who drain you, surround yourself with individuals who offer support and elevate your spirits. Seek out those who radiate positivity, for they are the same people who will cheer you on and inspire your personal growth.

💡 Exercise: Setting Boundaries

Take a moment to reflect on your life and relationships. Identify situations or individuals that deplete happiness and well-being. These could be people who constantly criticize you, drain your energy, or diminish your self-esteem.

Next, think about specific boundaries you can establish to protect your happiness and inner peace. These boundaries may include limiting your exposure to negative influences, communicating your needs more assertively, or distancing yourself from toxic individuals.

Write down these boundaries and commit to implementing them in your life. Practice asserting yourself in situations where your happiness is at stake and remind yourself that your well-being is a top priority. Over time, you'll find that setting healthy boundaries empowers you to take control of your happiness and reduces the influence of negativity from others.

SET WORK BOUNDARIES FOR A HEALTHIER YOU

*"Boundaries are how we communicate how we
want to be treated to the world."*
—Brené Brown

Recognize that boundaries are crucial in your professional life, just as they are in your personal life. No one is on their deathbed wishing they had spent more time at the office.

As you navigate your work environment, remember that establishing boundaries is acceptable and necessary for your well-being.

- No, you shouldn't have to put work over your health and family.
- No, you are not obligated to respond to work emails at midnight.
- No, you should not tolerate workplace harassment or bullying.

On the flip side:

- Yes, you should advocate for yourself and your needs.
- Yes, you should speak up and share valuable insights in meetings, your voice and opinion matter.
- Yes, you should create meaningful, trust-based connections with colleagues.

Remember this critical life lesson: We teach people how to treat us. *Boundaries are how we communicate how we want to be treated.* Healthy work boundaries promote well-being and a more respectful and balanced work environment.

💡 Exercise: Recognizing Unmet Needs and Setting Boundaries

- Begin by reflecting on your work life. Identify a specific situation or person that consistently leaves you exhausted and frustrated. This could be an ongoing project, a demanding colleague, or excessive work-related responsibilities.

- Acknowledge the need to establish boundaries with this situation or individual. Start with a small, manageable step, but maintain firmness in your decision.
- Choose one boundary that you can implement starting today. For instance, you might decide to wait to check work emails after 6 pm or during weekends.
- Commit to this boundary and communicate it clearly to those involved if necessary. Remember that setting boundaries is about prioritizing your well-being and promoting a healthier work-life balance.

By identifying and addressing the areas where your needs are not being met and taking deliberate steps to set boundaries, you can regain control over your work life and reduce feelings of exhaustion and frustration.

"My life underwent a profound transformation when I shifted my focus from what I wished to avoid and cultivated a mindset focused on actively pursuing what I wanted from life."

–Lan Phan

FOCUS ON THE GOOD

Where our eyes go, our body follows.

To invite more positivity into your life, center your focus on the good.

Always choose faith over fear and hope over despair.

While effort and hard work are required, they thrive when nurtured by unwavering self-belief and faith.

The path to self-belief starts with training your mind to uncover the positive amidst the darkest circumstances. Here are several methods to cultivate this:

- Gratitude Journal: Initiate a daily gratitude journal. List three things you're thankful for daily, even in challenging situations.
- Positive Affirmations: Compose a series of affirmations that resonate with you. Repeat them daily, especially when doubt or difficulty arises.
- Mindful Observation: Dedicate a few moments each day to mindful observation. Inhale, exhale, and observe your surroundings. Identify and appreciate the beauty or positivity in what you see, hear, or feel.
- Positive Media Consumption: Alter your media consumption habits. Seek uplifting news stories or content that inspires you. Limit exposure to harmful or distressing news when possible.
- Challenge Negative Thoughts: When you dwell on negative thoughts, interrogate them. Explore whether a more positive perspective or a valuable lesson can be found.
- Acts of Kindness: Participate in random acts of kindness. Spreading goodness to others can create a positive ripple effect and enhance positivity.
- Visualization: Dedicate a few minutes daily to visualize your goals and dreams as if they've already come to fruition. This practice reinforces a positive mindset and keeps your aspirations at the forefront.

Remember that nurturing a positive mindset is a journey that demands both time and practice. Exercise patience with yourself and remain steadfast in your commitment. As time unfolds, you'll discover that seeing the positive in every circumstance ultimately shapes your reality for the better.

LOVE YOUR FLAWS

"Once you've accepted your flaws, no one can use them against you."
—Peter Dinklage

What if we celebrated our perceived "flaws" and saw them as strengths? And instead of shrouding these flaws in the darkness, what if we illuminated them for all to see?

Once you've learned to love your flaws, no one can use them as a weapon. That includes yourself.

Living in the shadow of shame leads us to avoid meaningful connections, vulnerability, and community support—all essential for personal growth and flourishing.

What aspects of yourself have you concealed or felt ashamed of? By bringing them into the light, their power over you diminishes. We can simultaneously nurture self-love while striving for self-improvement. Feelings of self-loathing and shame benefit no one.

Once you've mastered the art of loving your imperfections, they cease to be ammunition in anyone's arsenal, including your own. Embracing your authentic self becomes the greatest gift you can bestow upon yourself.

When you learn to love yourself as you are, you'll witness a transformation in the world around you.

💡 Exercise: Reflecting on Personal Growth

Take a moment to explore what aspects of yourself may have evoked feelings of shame or embarrassment. It could be a past mistake that still lingers in your thoughts or is related to your age or how you perceive your physical appearance, such as the weight around your midsection. Identify these perceived "flaws."

Now, consider the transformative power of embracing and loving these facets of yourself, even as you actively engage in personal development and growth. What if you could embark on a journey of self-improvement without the burden of self-loathing?

Take some time to ponder these questions and envision how your life might change if you approached personal growth with self-compassion and acceptance.

THIS TOO SHALL PASS

"Every storm runs out of rain."
—Maya Angelou

In challenging moments, remember that this, too, shall pass. Resist the temptation to dwell within the tunnel of negativity; instead, consistently gravitate towards the light.

Personally, for me, moving toward the light means deepening my connection with my faith and God. For you, it could entail aligning with the Universe, science, reasoning, or nurturing the belief in your capabilities. Regardless of your chosen terminology, always move towards the light.

Throughout history, light has always prevailed over darkness. Remember that.

And when things get dark and overcast, never forget that every storm runs out of rain. Sunshine is near.

💡 Exercise: Cultivating a List of Uplifting Influences

- Begin by reflecting on the sources of light in your life – the people and things that consistently uplift you, bring joy or inspire positivity.
- Create a list of ten items, including individuals, activities, or objects that positively impact your well-being. Consider many aspects, such as personal relationships, hobbies, places, or favorite books or quotes.
- After compiling your list, take a moment to write a brief note next to each item, explaining why it brings light into your life. Reflect on the specific qualities or moments that make these sources of positivity meaningful to you.
- Keep your list in a readily accessible place, whether it's a physical journal, a digital document, or even a note on your smartphone.

- When you encounter challenging or dark moments, take a few minutes to revisit your list. Allow the positive memories and associations tied to each item to illuminate your mindset.
- Choose one item from your list and incorporate it into your day or week, even during difficult times. This could involve reaching out to a supportive friend, engaging in a favorite hobby, or revisiting a beloved book or quote.
- Journal Your Experience: Document how revisiting your list and engaging with these sources of light affects your mood and perspective during challenging moments. Note any insights or shifts in your emotional state.
- Reflect and Adapt: Over time, periodically revisit and update your list as new sources of light emerge in your life. Adjust your choices based on evolving circumstances and personal growth.

By cultivating this list of uplifting influences, you'll create a valuable resource for finding light amidst darkness and fostering resilience during challenging times.

STOP FEEDING YOUR FEARS

"Too many of us are not living our dreams because we are living our fears."
—Les Brown

Rather than feeding your fears, what if you nourished your soul with hope and love?

Many of us aren't chasing our dreams because we are trapped in the grip of our fears.

What if you surrounded yourself with individuals who genuinely believe in your capabilities? Those who inspire and bolster your spirit?

What if you began to invest in your potential instead of doubting yourself?

Stop feeding your fears and embark on a journey of unwavering faith and belief in yourself.

Feel the fear but do it anyway. Courage is not the absence of fear, it is taking action despite it.

💡 Exercise: Shifting from Fear to Positive Outlook

- Begin by identifying one specific thing currently causing you fear or anxiety. It could be related to a situation, a decision, or an upcoming event.
- Instead of dwelling on potential adverse outcomes, shift your perspective. Ask yourself, "What can I gain from this situation?"
- Create a list of these positive outcomes, no matter how small or insignificant they may seem. Consider various angles and possibilities, and let your imagination explore the potential benefits.
- Now, concentrate on the solutions and opportunities the situation presents rather than fixating on the problems or uncertainties.
- Challenge yourself to develop at least three potential solutions or actions to help you achieve those positive outcomes.

- Reflect on the newfound perspective you've gained from focusing on the positive aspects and solutions. How has it changed your perception of the situation?
- Create an affirmation or mantra that embodies this shift in thinking. For example, "I embrace the positive possibilities and solutions in every situation."

By consistently practicing this exercise, you'll develop a proactive mindset that empowers you to confront fear with optimism and focus on the potential for positive outcomes in any situation.

EMBRACE FAILURE

"You miss 100% of the shots you don't take."
—Wayne Gretzky

Stop being paralyzed by fear because you're afraid to fail. Understand that failure is not the opposite of success; it's a part of the journey towards success.

No one is born a master at anything. Every expert was once a beginner. Failing doesn't define you as a failure; it signifies that you took a chance on yourself and tried.

I call that a victory.

You're going to fail at times, and that's perfectly fine. Enjoy the ride. Learn from the experience. Pivot, adjust your course. Try again. Just take that first step towards getting better at whatever you want.

I'll emphasize this point because it's worth reiterating, don't let the fear of failure hold you back. Instead, fear not growing because you didn't believe in yourself enough to take that leap of faith. Fear being in the same place you are today, a decade from now, simply because you didn't believe in yourself enough to try.

💡 Exercise: Discovering Inspiration in Unconventional Success Stories

- Begin by conducting an online search using keywords like "individuals who struggled in school but achieved success" or "underestimated athletes who excelled later." You'll uncover a treasure trove of stories about prominent figures who initially faced setbacks or went unnoticed in their early years.
- As you explore these stories, pay close attention to the journeys of renowned athletes, entrepreneurs, and innovators who faced challenges or underperformance during their initial pursuits.

- Select at least two or three stories that resonate with you the most. Take notes on the key takeaways from each narrative, such as the obstacles they overcame, their determination, and their eventual achievements.
- Reflect on the similarities between your challenges and the struggles these individuals face. How do their experiences parallel your journey?
- Consider how these stories can serve as a source of motivation and encouragement for your personal goals and aspirations. Identify the lessons you can draw from their experiences.
- Create a list of actionable steps or strategies you can apply based on the insights gained from these success stories.
- When you encounter self-doubt or feel disheartened by setbacks, revisit the stories and insights you've gathered. Use them as a reminder that even the most accomplished individuals once faced obstacles similar to your own.

"This 'hustle harder' culture is getting really old.
I want you to know this:
you don't have to be productive
100% of the time.
Life isn't a race to see
who can do the most in a day.
It's a marathon, and sometimes
you need a rest day."

–Lan Phan

SOMETIMES WE NEED TO TAKE A BREAK

"It's okay to be a glowstick.
Sometimes, we break before we shine."
—Jadah Sellner

I get where you're coming from—the exhaustion, the stress, and the burnout. Trust me, I've been there too.

There are days when I just want to stay snuggled up in bed and not face the world. On those days, my attempt at motivation often involves watching episodes of Hoarders to kickstart my cleaning spree. Strange, right? But let's be honest, it usually doesn't work out as planned. Instead, I dive deep into the rabbit hole of videos featuring 20-year-old productivity gurus and wonder why I'm less effortlessly together than they seem. In case you're wondering, I'm writing this in my PJs.

I hear you; this "hustle harder" culture can quickly get old. Sometimes, we crave a little less hustle and a lot more chill. And guess what? That's perfectly okay.

I want you to know this: You don't have to be productive 100% of the time. Life isn't a race to see who can do the most in a day. It's a marathon, and sometimes you need a rest day. We all need those moments of rest, mental health days, and even those days when we just feel blah.

But here's the silver lining: it's all part of the journey. Your time to shine is still on its way, and sometimes, we need to break a little before we can truly dazzle.

So spending a day watching bad reality shows and lounging in bed is alright—we've all been there. Remember not to make it an everyday thing: it's a pause, not a habit. You have got goals to chase, which takes effort, but know it's also okay to take a day off now and then.

Keep shining bright, Raindrops.

💡 Exercise: Embracing Breaks and Shining Brighter

- Reflect on Your Feelings: Take a moment to reflect on your current state of mind. Are you feeling tired, stressed, or burnt out? Do you ever find yourself caught in the "hustle harder" culture, pressuring yourself constantly to be productive? Note down your thoughts and emotions.

- Identify Your Go-To Escapes: Think about how you cope with these feelings. What are your go-to activities or distractions when you need a break or a mental breather? Is it binge-watching TV shows, scrolling through social media, or something else entirely? Jot them down.

- Explore Your Motivation: Consider how these activities impact your motivation and well-being. Do they genuinely recharge you, or do you feel unproductive or even more stressed? Reflect on your experiences.

- Define Your Boundaries: Establish clear boundaries for yourself. Determine when it's okay to take a break and enjoy those "blah" days, and identify when you should challenge yourself to get back on track with your goals and responsibilities. Write down these boundaries.

- Set Realistic Goals: List some practical, achievable goals for your productive and restful days. What can you accomplish during those days when you feel motivated and energized? What's an acceptable level of relaxation when you're taking a break? Define your expectations.

- Create a "Shine Bright" Mantra: Develop a personal mantra that encourages you to embrace productivity and rest. For example, "I honor my need for rest and embrace my moments of motivation. Both are essential for my growth."

- Apply Your Insights: Apply your boundaries and goals over the next few weeks. When you need a break, indulge in your chosen activity, but do so mindfully. When it's time to return to work, remember your goals and mantra to rekindle your motivation.

By practicing this exercise, you'll become more mindful of your need for rest and productivity, finding a harmonious balance that allows you to shine brightly while embracing those occasional moments of respite.

DO HARD THINGS

"You Earn Self-Respect by Doing Hard Things Daily."
—Jordan Peterson

Do you find yourself constantly seeking validation from others? Have you made life choices, from what you wear, car you drive, to more significant decisions like your career choice, hoping to gain attention, respect, or approval from external sources? Chances are, like many of us, the answer is yes. Maybe it's your parents, significant other, boss, or neighbors—we've all been down that road.

But let me share a powerful truth: The most crucial validation you need in your life is your own. Self-respect is the cornerstone of your journey, and it begins with you.

Here's a Roadmap to Earn and Cultivate Self-Respect

- Honor Your Commitments: Start by honoring the promises you make to yourself. Whether waking up at 5 a.m., launching a business, or embracing a healthier lifestyle, you reinforce your self-respect when you keep these commitments. Breaking them erodes them.
- Embrace Challenges: Consider your self-worth as a muscle—it grows stronger when you challenge it. Engage in hard tasks daily, pushing your limits and nurturing your grit. Each obstacle you overcome is a step toward a more robust self-respect.
- Master Your Emotions: Don't let emotions dictate your life. Instead, learn to control them. When you steer your feelings, you're charting the course of your life. It's your power to wield.
- Focus on Your Strengths: Recognize your strengths and leverage them. While addressing weaknesses is essential, nurturing your strengths amplifies your self-respect. It's the acknowledgment of your unique abilities.
- Persist, Don't Quit: Above all, never give up. Self-respect isn't handed out; it's earned. It comes from facing challenges head-on, overcoming hurdles, and persevering through life's ups and downs.

Remember, self-respect isn't a gift; it's an accomplishment. It arises from the daily pursuit of personal growth, the commitment to your word, and the unwavering dedication to keep moving forward. Your journey is a testament to your self-respect, built one day and one promise kept at a time.

SPEAK KINDLY

"If speaking kindly to plants helps them grow, imagine
what speaking kindly to humans can do."
—Robin Sharma

Let's talk about the incredible power of our words. You see, they possess the remarkable ability to either uplift or diminish those around us.

But here's the thing—it's not just about how we speak to others; it's also about how we talk to ourselves. Yes, you read that right. Be as kind to yourself as you are to your dearest friends.

Remember, our words and thoughts are like the architects of our destiny. So, choose them with care, my friend. Choose kindness and positivity, and watch the world transform into a brighter and more beautiful place.

💡 Exercise: The Power of Positive Self-Talk

Let's embark on a transformative exercise that will shift your perspective and boost your positivity.

Start by observing your thoughts for at least 10 minutes. Pay close attention to the nature of these thoughts. Are they predominantly positive or tinged with negativity? Take mental notes or jot them down if it helps.

As you monitor your thoughts, look for negative self-talk or critical comments you might be making about yourself.

When you catch a negative thought or self-commentary, pause. Here's the game-changer: consciously reframe it from a negative to a positive perspective. For example, if you catch yourself thinking, "I can't do this," flip it to "I'll give it my best shot, and I can learn from it."

Continue this process during your 10-minute thought-monitoring session. Each time you identify a negative thought, challenge it and replace it with a more positive and constructive one.

Extend this exercise into your daily routine. Dedicate a few minutes each day to consciously monitor and reframe your thoughts. Over time, you'll notice a shift towards a more optimistic mindset.

Remember, this exercise is a powerful tool to foster self-compassion and enhance overall well-being. By actively reshaping your thoughts from negative to positive, you'll open the door to a brighter, more optimistic outlook on life.

LOVE YOURSELF

*"Loving ourselves through the process of owning our story
is the bravest thing we will ever do."*
—Brené Brown

To grow, we must share our story, shed the weight of shame and regret, and most importantly, learn to love ourselves through it all. It's a journey, my friend, and it's worth every step.

You see, dwelling in shame, regret, or constant worry might seem like something to do to pass the time, but let's be honest—it only leads to unhappiness. It's like running on a treadmill, lots of effort, but you're not really going anywhere.

Now, here's the game-changer: self-love. It is a beautiful, challenging, and potent thing.

Here's the irony of life—the more you embrace and love yourself just as you are, flaws and all, the more love flows into your life from others. It's like a ripple effect of positivity and kindness.

So, my dear, own your story, let go of that unnecessary baggage, and embark on the most beautiful love affair you'll ever experience—the one with yourself. It's a lifetime journey, and you're worth it.

💡 Exercise: The Journey to Self-Love

Let's embark on a transformative exercise designed to help you embrace your story, release shame and regret, and cultivate self-love—the most beautiful gift you can give to yourself.

Take a few moments to reflect on your life journey, the experiences that have shaped you, and the lessons you've learned. Embrace your story, acknowledging that it's essential to who you are today.

As you reflect, pinpoint any lingering feelings of shame, regret, or worry that may be holding you back or causing you distress. Be honest with yourself about these emotions.

Visualize yourself releasing these negative emotions one by one. Imagine them as heavy weights that you can set down and leave behind. Take a deep breath and exhale, symbolizing the release of each burden.

Create a list of affirmations that promote self-love and self-acceptance. For example, "I love and accept myself just as I am," or "I am worthy of love and happiness." Choose affirmations that resonate with you.

Stand before a mirror and look deeply into your eyes. While gazing at your reflection, repeat your chosen self-love affirmations aloud. Speak them with sincerity and conviction, letting them sink into your heart.

Integrate your chosen self-love affirmations into your daily routine. Revisit them in the morning or before bedtime to reinforce self-love and self-acceptance.

Commit to engaging in acts of self-kindness regularly. This could involve self-care practices, setting healthy boundaries, or simply treating yourself with the same love and compassion you offer others.

After a few weeks of practicing self-love, revisit your journal. Reflect on your progress and celebrate your journey toward embracing your story and cultivating self-love.

This exercise is powerful for nurturing self-love, letting go of negative emotions, and embracing your unique life journey. Remember, your relationship with yourself is the foundation for all other relationships, so cherish it and watch how it positively impacts your overall well-being.

HEAL YOUR HATE

*"The real flex is healing yourself without becoming
like those who traumatized you."*
—Unknown

True strength lies in healing yourself without adopting the traits of those
who cause you harm. Love has always been the antidote for hate—a force
capable of transmuting darkness into light, mending wounds, and healing
broken hearts.

Now, I want you to understand this—holding onto negative emotions such
as hate, jealousy, and resentment doesn't just harm those around you; it
corrupts your very being from the inside out. It's akin to ingesting a poison
that gradually consumes you, leaving its mark before you speak. Perhaps
you've crossed paths with individuals whose discontent and resentment
are palpable, shrouding their environment and draining the vitality from
a room as they enter.

But here's the secret: choosing love doesn't mean you have to accept bad
behavior in your life. Instead, it means you rise above it. It's a refusal to
allow negativity to define your character. It's a commitment to radiate light
in a world shrouded in darkness. It means not becoming like those who
hurt you in your healing process.

You possess a strength greater than any adversity you've faced. Always
bear that in mind. Liberating yourself from the cycle of negativity, dear
Raindrops, is your path to freedom. Embrace love not as a symbol of
vulnerability but as a bold act, a radiant beacon of hope that lights up a
brighter world."

💡 Exercise: Conduct an honest assessment of your relationships with others.

Take a moment to recognize whether you are harboring negative emotions
such as hate, jealousy, or resentment. Are you unintentionally perpetuating

past wounds inflicted upon you onto those you hold dear? If you are trapped in a cycle of reliving past pain and believe it is detrimental to yourself and your loved ones, seeking a way to break free from this pattern is essential.

Understand that clinging to negative emotions adversely affects those in your vicinity and, perhaps even more significantly, erodes your inner peace and overall well-being. It's akin to carrying a heavy burden that gradually saps your vitality. Contact a friend for support or consider seeking therapy to facilitate healing. In doing so, you can release these emotions without perpetuating the cycle of harm inflicted by others.

Letting go of these emotions and embracing love doesn't imply that you must tolerate or accept bad behavior from others. Instead, it signifies your choice to transcend negativity. You are deciding not to allow it to shape your identity or your actions. Dedicate yourself to opting for love over negativity in your daily life. This entails practicing forgiveness, understanding, and empathy, even in challenging circumstances.

FORGIVE YOURSELF

*"Forgive yourself for the times you disappointed yourself, for the times
you were in the wrong, for the times you felt like you weren't enough,
for the things you said out loud in anger, for the past mistakes you've
made, for the times you could have been more empathetic, for the
times you've realized you were the toxic one, for the lessons you learned
a little too late, for the times you didn't stand up for yourself."*
—Unknown

Many of us have often been taught the importance of forgiving others, but
have you extended the same compassion to yourself?

Indeed, our life's journey is filled with valuable lessons. We stumble, make
mistakes, and learn from them. Each misstep becomes an opportunity
for personal growth, a chance to turn pain into progress. Amidst this, a
pearl of profound wisdom should never be overlooked—the art of treating
ourselves gently and forgiving ourselves.

My mother imparted to me the incredible power of forgiveness. When we
grant ourselves forgiveness, we unburden our hearts from the chains of
hurt, anger, and resentment that may have taken root. It's a transformative
act that liberates us.

So, here's your gentle reminder: Forgive yourself, not to forget, but as
a catalyst for learning, growth, and change. Embrace the beauty of
self-compassion, and let it be the cornerstone of your journey.

💡 Exercise: The Liberating Act of Self-Forgiveness

What guilt are you clinging on to? You start the healing process by for-
giving yourself. Remind yourself that you are loved. You have always been
loved. But first, you must love yourself. Let's embark on a transformative
exercise to release the burdens of guilt and embrace the profound healing
power of self-forgiveness. Remember, you are worthy of love, especially
your own.

Take a few deep, calming breaths to center yourself.

Begin by delving into your heart and identifying any lingering feelings of guilt or self-blame. These may be related to past mistakes, missed opportunities, or moments when you didn't meet your expectations. Acknowledge these emotions without judgment.

Grab a journal or a piece of paper. Write down the specific instances or aspects of your life where you're holding on to guilt. Be honest and thorough in your reflections.

Take a moment to forgive yourself with each item you've listed. Write a heartfelt forgiveness statement for each, addressing yourself with kindness and understanding. For example, "I forgive myself for _____. I understand that I am human and make mistakes. I release this burden of guilt and choose to learn and grow from it."

Create a list of self-love affirmations to reinforce your worthiness. These affirmations should remind you of your inherent value and the love that surrounds you. For instance, "I am worthy of love, including my own," or "I choose to love and accept myself unconditionally."

Close your eyes and visualize each piece of guilt transforming into a feather-light balloon. As you release it, watch these balloons gently float away, carrying your responsibility with them, leaving you feeling lighter and freer.

Perform an act of self-compassion. It could be as simple as a warm, soothing bath, a walk in nature, or spending quality time doing something you love.

As you gradually release guilt and embrace self-forgiveness, celebrate your growing sense of lightness and freedom. Every step toward self-love is a step toward a more joyful and fulfilling life.

Remember, my dear friend, self-forgiveness is a gift to yourself and a profound source of healing and growth. You create space for love, compassion, and personal transformation to flourish by releasing guilt.

STOP MAKING YOURSELF SMALL

"Stop shrinking yourself to fit into places you've outgrown."
—Lori Deschene

Let's talk about the things I've been told at work:
"Stay in your lane."
"You're not a very good writer."
"You need to lead from the front."
"I'd rather you not speak up at meetings."
"I'll present your deck because you're not a natural public speaker."
"You're not ready for leadership."

Once, a company CEO I had worked with advised me to 'stay in my lane' when he perceived I was becoming overly ambitious. In less than a year, I resigned without another job in place.

Funny thing: A year later, that same company approached me and requested my consulting services. I submitted a proposal, only for them to realize they couldn't afford my services.

Betting on yourself is scary. Believing in yourself can be difficult.

But you know what's truly scary? Staying in places that don't appreciate or celebrate you, allowing others to make you feel small, waking up five years from now, and being exactly where you are today.

Stop making yourself small to accommodate weak, small-minded people. Their inability to see your worth does not diminish your inherent value.

Deep within you resides a wellspring of talent, untapped potential, and remarkable strength. Place your faith in yourself, invest in your capabilities, and acquire the wisdom to leave when respect is not reciprocated. As you learn to honor and value yourself, you will ascend beyond any limitations that others may attempt to impose upon you.

Your life's journey is an expedition of self-discovery, a quest to recognize your intrinsic worth and harness your innate power. It's a journey toward becoming your authentic self and the most genuine version of you.

Exercise: Cultivating Self-Respect and Self-Honoring

Let's embark on a profound exercise aimed at nurturing self-respect and embracing self-honoring practices. This journey will help you recognize your inherent worth and prioritize your well-being.

Begin by reflecting on the concept of self-respect. Consider what it means to you and why it's crucial for your well-being. Write down your thoughts and feelings.

Identify areas where you may have neglected your self-respect or failed to honor yourself. These might be situations where you compromised your values or neglected self-care.

Craft a personal pledge or commitment to yourself, outlining specific actions and boundaries that reflect your commitment to self-respect and self-honor. For example, "I pledge to prioritize self-care by dedicating at least 30 minutes each day to activities that rejuvenate my mind and body."

Define clear boundaries in your personal and professional life. Write down situations where you need to establish or reinforce boundaries to protect your self-respect.

Develop a self-compassion ritual that you can practice regularly. This could include meditation, journaling, or affirmations that remind you of your worth and value.

Identify any past instances where you compromised your self-respect or failed to honor yourself. Practice self-forgiveness and release any lingering guilt or regret.

Consider sharing your self-respect pledge with a trusted friend or mentor who can hold you accountable and support your journey.

Remember that self-respect is the foundation of a fulfilling and balanced life. By engaging in this exercise and prioritizing self-respect, you're nurturing your well-being and honoring the unique and valuable individual you are.

MOVE THROUGH NEGATIVE EMOTIONS

*"If it's not gonna matter in 5 years—don't spend
more than 5 minutes being upset about it."*
—Unknown

Listen up. Life is too short to stew over past injustices or let minor annoyances control your emotions. Stop giving a shit about trivial things. I'm not saying you shouldn't feel these emotions—you absolutely should. However, here's the key: Do not permit them to take up residence in your mind. Do not grant them the power to spoil your day or tarnish your life.

When you allow negative emotions to linger, they multiply like weeds in a garden, suffocating the beauty within. They don't confine themselves to your thoughts alone; they seep into your physical and mental well-being.

Residing beneath a perpetual cloud of negativity will inevitably deteriorate your overall well-being. It's akin to a gradual poison, eroding your vitality. Living with such emotions is akin to being consumed from within.

Yet here's the pivotal truth—you can alter this course. You harbor the strength to let go, to release those emotions, and to cultivate a positive environment where you can flourish and thrive.

So do not surrender control of your life to negativity. Do not allow it to erode your happiness. Instead, focus on the positive aspects of your existence and thrive.

💡 Exercise: The Five-Minute Emotion Release

During this dedicated time, allow yourself to fully embrace any negative emotions you may be experiencing, big or small. Permit yourself to feel anger, frustration, sadness, or whatever you're going through.

Limit this emotional release to just five minutes. Use a timer if needed. During these five minutes, let the emotions flow freely. Don't suppress them or judge yourself for feeling this way.

As you experience these emotions, remember that they don't define you. Think of them as borrowed emotions, passing through you like a temporary storm. They are here to teach you something, but they do not belong to you.

Once the five minutes are up, consciously release these emotions. Imagine them leaving your body, like a heavy cloud dissipating into the sky. Visualize yourself letting go and making space for positivity and clarity.

Conclude by affirming your control over your emotions. Say something like, "I can acknowledge and release my emotions healthily. I am in control of how I feel."

Practice this five-minute emotional release whenever negative emotions arise. Over time, you'll become more skilled at managing your emotions and maintaining your emotional well-being.

BE PRESENT

"You make your life hard by always being in your head. Life is simple. Get out of your head and get into the moment."
—Sylvester McNutt

There is only this moment.
Center yourself.
Breathe deeply.

Often, we find ourselves grappling with inner demons, trapped by the echoes of the past or entangled in the uncertainty of the future.

But here's the profound truth: The present moment has always been the only thing that truly exists.

Breathe in this moment, my friend. Inhale deeply and let in all the hope and possibilities before you. As you exhale, release the weight of yesterday's burdens and tomorrow's anxiety.

You are here now, and that is where your strength lies.

In this moment, you can redefine your path, rewrite your story, and rediscover your purpose. The past may have shaped you, but the present is where you craft the rest of your life.

Life is not a race to the finish line. It is a journey to becoming who you were always meant to be.

Seize the moment.

Embrace it with open arms, and let it guide you on your extraordinary trip.

💡 Exercise: The Art of Present Moment Awareness

Let's embark on a journey to strengthen your ability to stay present and fully engaged in the beauty of each moment.

Find Your Sanctuary: Select a quiet and comfortable space where you won't be disturbed during practice. It could be a cozy corner of your home or a peaceful spot in nature.

Body Scan Meditation: Start with a simple body scan meditation. Close your eyes, take a few deep breaths, and bring your attention to your toes. Gradually move your focus through your body, noting any tension or sensations. This practice grounds you in the physical sensations of the present moment.

Engage Your Senses: Spend a few minutes engaging your senses. Close your eyes and listen to the sounds around you—the rustling leaves, the hum of life. Open your eyes and focus on a single object, observing its details. Inhale deeply, taking in any scents in the air. Touch a nearby surface and feel its texture.

Mindful Breathing: Shift your attention to your breath. Breathe naturally and observe each inhalation and exhalation. If your mind starts to wander, gently guide it back to the sensation of your breath.

Release Judgment: As you practice, allow your thoughts to come and go without judgment. If worries or distractions arise, acknowledge them and return your focus to the present moment.

Daily Mindful Moments: Throughout your day, set reminders on your phone or use everyday cues, like opening a door or taking a sip of water, to bring your awareness back to the present moment. Take a brief pause and engage your senses.

Nature Connection: Spend time in nature regularly, whether it's a walk in the park, a hike in the woods, or simply sitting in your garden. Nature is an influential teacher of presence.

Mindful Eating: During one meal each day, practice mindful eating. Pay close attention to the flavors, textures, and sensations as you savor each bite. Put away distractions like phones or TV.

Remember, the journey to presence is ongoing, and there's no destination to reach—only a way of being to cultivate. By practicing these moments of presence, you'll gradually infuse your life with greater awareness, gratitude, and a deeper connection to the beauty of each passing moment.

LEARN FROM FAILURE

"Success is walking from failure with no loss of enthusiasm."
—Winston Churchill

No one teaches us that failure is just as important as winning. No one celebrates the loser. Yet everyone fails and loses at some point in their life. Yes, even the people we consider as winners: the G.O.A.T.s, MVPs, billionaires. The truth is that our failures can become an accelerant to success.

Failure is not a weight that anchors us down; it's a springboard that propels us forward. It's not a permanent state but a temporary condition where growth and learning occur.

What if we could strip away the fear that often shrouds failure? What if we viewed it not as a stumbling block but as a steppingstone to our dreams?

I often think of Spanx CEO Sara Blakely's story about her father gathering the kids around the dinner table and having them share their story of a failure for the day. After each child recounted their story, everyone would cheer them on. I can't help but think that Sara's success and fearlessness as an entrepreneur were nurtured by that environment where failure was not a dreaded foe but something to be encouraged as a path to self-development.

My dear friends, failure is one of the most powerful learning tools you'll ever have. It's your classroom, mentor, and guide on the journey to success. Every misstep and setback carry within it the seeds of knowledge and resilience.

The key is taking the fear out of failure. Instead, see it as a powerful learning tool. Failure is one of the most powerful learning tools you will ever have.

Embrace failure not as a defeat but as a courageous step towards your dreams. With each stumble, you are one step closer to soaring to new heights.

🔦 Exercise: Recalling Your Last Setback

Consider your most recent setback or failure. Now, delve into self-reflection with these guiding questions:

What Lessons Were Gained? Reflect on what valuable lessons or insights you acquired from this experience. How did it contribute to your personal growth or professional development?

Contemplate the steps you can take to enhance your performance or approach the next time you encounter a similar challenge. How can you apply these newfound lessons to your advantage?

Imagine a life where the fear of failure didn't hold you back. Envision the possibilities and opportunities that would open to you. How might this change your approach to future endeavors?

Allow this exercise to inspire your journey toward self-improvement and a fearless pursuit of your goals.

HUMILITY IS ADMIRABLE, DIMINISHING ONESELF, NOT SO MUCH

"Playing Humble will have you overlooked, underpaid, and underbooked."
—Alex Elle

This is a hard lesson I had to learn: There is a fine line between being humble and playing small, and it's high time we set the record straight.

Humility is a commendable quality, but diminishing oneself is not.

If you fail to take credit for your accomplishments and contributions, rest assured someone else will take the credit for you. While humility is a virtue, not valuing your input and not advocating for yourself can lead to being overlooked and underappreciated.

Yes, I said it.

Stop playing small because others may feel threatened by your potential. Stop staying in places that stifle your growth. And stop permitting others to claim credit for your hard-earned work.

Being humble does not mean diminishing your worth to appease others. Instead, it's about recognizing the inherent power within you and striving daily to become a better version of yourself. It's about acknowledging your efforts and contributions so others will recognize your achievements.

Being humble means recognizing that your actual competition is the person gazing back at you in the mirror.

Being humble means that belittling others does not make you better than anyone, it makes you an asshole.

Being humble means acknowledging that no great achievement is accomplished in isolation. I call this higher source "God," but you might refer to it as "AI," "your teammates," "community," or "science." Regardless of the name, no one succeeds entirely on their own.

Humility entails recognizing your greatness while appreciating the greatness in others.

Humility is aspiring to be your best self without seeking external validation.

Humility is about safeguarding your radiance from those who may attempt to eclipse it.

True humility doesn't entail diminishing your worth to conform to someone else's limited perception of you. It's about embracing the boundless power within and committing to a continual journey of self-improvement.

So, embrace your humility, but never let it be a veil that dims your light. Hold your head high, stand in your truth, and let your brilliance shine unapologetically.

💡 Exercise: Recognize Your Shine

Take a moment to acknowledge and celebrate your individuality. List five qualities, talents, or strengths that set you apart and make you exceptional. Embrace and revel in your awesomeness!

CULTIVATE EMPATHY

*"Empathy is seeing with the eyes of another, listening with the
ears of another, and feeling with the heart of another."*
—Alfred Adler

Empathy, the ability to comprehend and resonate with the emotions and thoughts of those around us, is a cornerstone of effective leadership. It's a lesson often learned through experience: life's disruptive events, tragedies, or personal adversities are powerful but unwanted teaching tools. Our capacity for empathy is usually limited to those who share our backgrounds, beliefs, and experiences.

Let me share my journey: In my early twenties, as a manager, I found it challenging to comprehend the struggles of my colleagues who were parents. Their inability to work late into the night or travel extensively, like I could, perplexed me. Yet life had its way of teaching me. As a parent now, I intimately understand the challenges working moms and dads face. To all the parents out there, I see you!

Recognizing my past shortcomings, I've committed to do better. I've realized that waiting to live others' shared experience before empathizing with them isn't the answer.

As leaders, it's our responsibility to bridge the gap, even when we can't walk in someone else's shoes. For instance, I'll never fully comprehend the experience of being a man, but I can use my eyes, ears, and heart to empathize with my male colleagues. I need to ask more questions, pause to truly listen, and cultivate a diverse network of connections and friendships to avoid a monolithic viewpoint.

In an age characterized by the ascent of AI, automation, and technology, let's not lose sight of the qualities that uniquely define us as humans:

Our innate aptitude for genuine human connections.
Our insatiable curiosity drives innovation.

Our capability to truly listen and understand.
Our readiness to empathize and forge meaningful relationships.
Our inherent kindness and compassion.

At the core of any organization lies its people, the heartbeat of its existence. It always has been and always will be. So, let's keep sight of our humanity. It's perfectly okay to be human, to experience emotions, and to grant others the same privilege. Empathy is, without a doubt, a superpower. It empowers us to become better workers, compassionate bosses, considerate clients, supportive spouses, true friends, and understanding parents. It is the vital thread that intricately weaves the fabric that brings people together.

💡 Exercise: Empathy Is Not Fixed; It Can Be Developed

You can cultivate empathy by being curious, stepping out of your comfort zone, receiving feedback, examining your biases, and walking in other people's shoes. Things you can try doing include:

- Spending time with people different from you and getting to know them. Ask questions and be present with them when you talk to them.
- Read and follow people from different backgrounds—religion, race, political persuasion, etc.
- Visit new places and countries, meet local people, and immerse yourself in their lifestyle.
- Ask for feedback from friends and family regarding your active listening skills. How can you improve?
- We all have biases, and they impact how we see the world. So, find opportunities to talk to people about what is important to them.

CLAIM YOUR WORTH

"Make sure you don't start seeing yourself through the eyes of those who don't value you. Know your worth even if they don't."
—Thema Davis

Stop waiting for someone to validate your existence. Your value doesn't decrease because someone doesn't see your worth.

Here's an uncomfortable truth: Not everyone is going to like you. I know, shocker. The good news is that there are over 8.1 billion other people on this planet. You're bound to find your tribe. Just keep looking. And for every person who doesn't see your value, at least a hundred will.

Until respect is returned, learn the art of distancing yourself from those who undermine your self-worth. Establish boundaries and refuse to justify their behavior. It is not your responsibility to endure unfair treatment.

Rather than internalizing their judgments, channel your energy into daily self-improvement. Embrace personal growth and remember that achieving success remains the most potent form of retribution.

💡 Exercise: Think of a Person Who Doesn't Like or Value You

Great. Now, think of five people who *do* appreciate and value you. Spend more time with the latter and less with the former.

HAVE FAITH

"EVERYTHING you are going through is preparing
YOU for what you asked for…"
—Siri Lindley

The challenges and hardships you've encountered along your life's journey have played an indispensable role in molding your resilience and wisdom. Always keep this truth close to your heart.

Maintaining a positive outlook can be daunting, especially when the world is unraveling. Yet, in these tumultuous moments, your faith should take center stage, even if it's as small as a mustard seed.

Remember, faith is an unwavering belief in the unseen, especially in the face of the present's uncertainties. This lies at its core. Faith and fear cannot coexist in the same space.

The choice is yours: Will you opt for faith, the driving force that propels you forward, or will you yield to fear, the burden that impedes your progress?

💡 Exercise: Cultivating Unshakeable Faith

Let's embark on a journey to nurture and strengthen your faith, even in the face of life's uncertainties. This exercise will help you embrace the power of belief and move beyond fear.

Reflect on your past experiences and the trials you've endured. Consider how these challenges have contributed to your personal growth and wisdom. Write down three significant life lessons you've learned through adversity.

Visualize a mustard seed, one of the tiniest seeds known to man. It symbolizes the smallest measure of faith capable of moving mountains. Imagine yourself holding this seed in your hand. Close your eyes and meditate on what this seed represents to you. How can this small but mighty seed inspire you to nurture your faith?

Examine areas where fear may be holding you back. It could be fear of failure, rejection, or the unknown. Identify one specific fear that you'd like to confront and overcome. Write it down.

Craft a positive affirmation that counters your chosen fear. For example, if you fear failure, your affirmation might be: "I embrace failure as a steppingstone to success." Repeat this affirmation aloud daily, ideally in the morning or before bedtime.

Remember, faith is a lifelong journey, and with dedication and practice, your faith can grow and flourish, guiding you toward a brighter and more resilient future.

STUMBLE

"Sometimes you must hurt in order to know, fall in order to grow, lose in order to gain because most of life's greatest lessons are learned through pain."
–Pain Nagato

Those challenging moments aren't indicators of failure; they are pivotal opportunities for growth and grit. They serve as invaluable lessons, imparting strength, and resilience, and exist to empower your personal development. You didn't falter; you emerged stronger. These trials were the essential steppingstones on your journey to becoming who you are today.

Imagine a child taking their first steps—each stumble and fall contributes to strengthening their muscles for the path ahead. The more they encounter hurdles, the more robust they become.

Remember, when you transform your mindset, you can transform your entire world. Change your thinking, change your life.

💡 Exercise: Strength Through Adversity

While no one actively seeks out pain and adversity, recollect a time when you experienced personal growth due to facing challenges.

How did that experience benefit you in the long run?
What skills did you develop?
How did this experience contribute to your personal growth and resilience?

Write down at least three lessons you gained. This exercise encourages you to recognize the strength and development that can arise from adversity and appreciate the valuable lessons learned.

BE PATIENT

One day, you'll understand why God made you wait.

One day, the wait will be worth it.

Here's my testament for those grappling with the uncertainties of today's world.

In my thirties, I left San Francisco, shattered by a painful breakup, and relocated to New York. Before moving, I had resigned from my stable, high-paying job without a backup plan, and for months, I was woefully unemployed. I felt as though I had hit rock bottom.

I sent out countless resumes and applications and was met with silence. It felt like my life was going nowhere, with no end in sight. Little did I realize it was the start of my journey, not the end.

I met my current husband, and we got married in our mid-thirties. At 40, I welcomed my daughter into the world, a blessing I had nearly given up on just a year prior due to infertility. More recently, I discovered my life's purpose after being let go from what I deemed my dream job, leading to establishing my dream company at the age of 45.

These experiences taught me that God's delays are not God's denial.

Keep going, for this is but the prologue of your story. It's not too late to start again. This is only the beginning for you. If you're unhappy with how your story is going, rewrite it. Just don't quit.

💡 Exercise: Embracing Patience and Rewriting Your Story

Take a few moments to think about your life journey and the challenges or uncertainties you may face.

Reflect on Your Journey:

> Reflect on your life journey and acknowledge past instances where patience and resilience have been crucial to your success or personal growth. Write about these experiences, highlighting the positive outcomes that emerged from your patience and determination.

Rewrite Your Story:

> Based on the inspiration from the passage and your reflections on your journey, create a vision of how you would like your current challenging situation to evolve. Describe the steps you can take to rewrite your story and overcome the challenges you face. Be specific and realistic about your action plan.

Set Goals and Commitments:

> Define clear goals and milestones that align with your vision for rewriting your story. Commit to taking action on these goals and hold yourself accountable for progress.

Regularly Review and Adjust:

> Dedicate time to regularly review your progress, celebrate small victories, and adjust your plan as needed. Draw inspiration from the passage whenever you encounter difficulties or uncertainties.

Offer support to others who may be facing their challenges, just as the passage encourages celebrating the progress of others.

This exercise encourages you to embrace patience, draw inspiration from your past resilience, and actively work toward rewriting your story when faced with challenges. By persistently moving forward and adapting to life's uncertainties, you can create a narrative that reflects your growth, resilience, and determination.

GROW THROUGH ADVERSITY

"They tried to bury us. They didn't know we were seeds."
—Dinos Christianopoulos

Let me say this clearly for the folks sitting in the back. Their inability to see your value does not decrease your worth. Not getting that promotion or raise or being selected for that project when you know you put in the work does not define you.

When I was younger, I would be devastated when I wasn't chosen—it didn't matter if it was work, love, or friendship. Frequently, I would be immobile with grief, wondering why I wasn't enough.

As I got older and wiser, I discovered this truth: I was created by God to grow and prosper. The fact that you were born and alive proves that you were chosen. Read that again.

However, a weak-minded few thrive on making others feel small. You should never let those who can't see your worth use their biased measuring stick to define your value.

Though some will try to destroy you, you were made to grow and prosper like a seed.

🔦 Exercise: Nourishing Your Self-Worth

This exercise aims to help you counteract moments when someone has made you feel insignificant by reaffirming your self-worth. You can cultivate a stronger sense of self-esteem and personal growth by identifying their mistakes in their assessment.

Recall a Past Experience: Take a moment to reflect on a specific incident or encounter in which someone made you feel small or underestimated your abilities. Recall the circumstances and emotions associated with that experience.

List Five Reasons They Were Wrong: In your journal, list five compelling reasons why the person who made you feel small was mistaken in their assessment. Consider your strengths, achievements, and qualities that contradict their negative perception of you. Be specific and detailed in your explanations.

Affirm Your Growth Potential: Remind yourself that, like a seed, you possess immense potential for growth and transformation. Write down a few sentences reaffirming your capacity for personal development and achieving your goals.

Reflect on Your Resilience: Contemplate how you've overcome challenges and setbacks in the past. Write about your resilience and adaptability, emphasizing how you've bounced back from difficult situations.

Acknowledge Your Accomplishments: List some of your significant achievements, both big and small, that reflect your capabilities and talents. Reflect on how these accomplishments demonstrate your worth and potential.

Future Growth Goals: Identify one or two areas in which you aspire to grow and develop. Write down actionable steps to nurture your growth in these areas.

Practice Self-Compassion: Recognize that everyone faces moments of doubt and criticism, but how you respond matters most. Offer yourself self-compassion and forgiveness for any lingering self-doubt stemming from past experiences.

Regularly Review and Reaffirm: Make it a habit to revisit the reasons why they were wrong and your affirmations of self-worth. Whenever you encounter self-doubt or negativity, refer to this exercise as a source of empowerment and self-assurance.

This exercise serves as a tool for building and fortifying your self-esteem. By identifying your strengths, achievements, and growth potential, you can counteract moments when others underestimate you, and like a resilient seed, continue to thrive and flourish in your life journey.

BETTER DAYS ARE AHEAD

*"What a wonderful thought that some of the best days
of our lives haven't even happened yet."*
–Anne Frank

Even in the darkest days, hope is the unwavering force that keeps us going. Amidst the heart of adversity, we find a beacon of hope, a reminder that brighter days await us and that the best days of our lives are still in front of us.

When we find ourselves amidst our trials and tribulations, it's easy to lose sight of the horizon and succumb to the weight of our worries and fears. We question if the sun will ever shine again.

When we are going through challenging moments, let us hold fast to this beautiful truth by Maya Angelou: "Every cloud eventually runs out of rain."

The storms that engulf us today inevitably make way for the sunshine of tomorrow. Just as dawn follows the darkest hour of the night, better days unfailingly emerge after our hardships.

The universe possesses a remarkable equilibrium, rewarding our endurance and patience with joy, growth, and transformation moments.

Each obstacle we confront, every tear we shed, and every challenge we conquer weaves a thread into the intricate design of our lives. These experiences mold our character, strengthen our spirit, and prepare us for the extraordinary days yet to unfold. Emerging from adversity, we stand stronger, wiser, and more resilient, poised to savor life's blessings with profound gratitude.

In moments of darkness, hold steadfast to the wondrous possibilities that await: a future brimming with opportunities, adventures, and profound happiness beyond imagination. As we navigate life's turbulent currents, remember that we forge a path toward the best days of our existence—days that extend their arms to us, ready to reveal their splendor and enchantment at the appointed time.

So, when the world feels dark, and uncertainty casts its shadow, find solace in the knowledge that brighter days are on the horizon. Embrace each hardship as a steppingstone toward the greatness that lies ahead, for the most magnificent chapters of your life are yet to be written, and they promise joy, purpose, and fulfillment beyond your wildest dreams.

💡 Exercise: Nurturing Hope and Resilience

Reflect on Past Challenges: Take a moment to think about a significant challenge or adversity you've faced. It could be a personal, professional, or emotional challenge.

Identify Lessons and Growth: Consider what valuable lessons you learned from this adversity and how they contributed to your personal growth and resilience. List at least three specific lessons or insights gained from that experience.

Create a Vision Board: Using magazines, printed images, or digital tools, create a vision board representing your future aspirations and the better days you envision. Include pictures and words that inspire hope, joy, and personal growth.

Share Your Journey: If you're comfortable, share your reflections and vision board with someone you trust, a friend, or a supportive community. Discuss how you plan to navigate challenges while keeping your focus on the brighter days that lie ahead.

This exercise encourages you to recognize the transformative power of hope and resilience in the face of adversity. It also helps you envision a future filled with opportunities and moments of profound happiness while learning from past challenges.

THE TRANSFORMATIVE POWER OF GRATITUDE

*"Acknowledging the good that you already have in
your life is the foundation for all abundance.'*
—Eckhart Tolle

Positive psychology has illuminated a profound truth: gratitude is a shield against negativity, an elixir that can boost your happiness by a remarkable 25%. It has the astonishing capacity to rewire your brain, dismantle the fortress of stress, revitalize your body, enhance your slumber, and fortify the bonds within your relationships.

In times of adversity, when life's challenges cast their long shadows, the value of gratitude may appear paradoxical. However, during these tumultuous periods, gratitude assumes even greater importance.

But why is this emphasis on gratitude so vital? The answer lies in a fundamental principle of life: What we focus on has the power to expand and flourish.

If you aspire to craft an existence brimming with abundance, your focal point should invariably be abundance. Contemplate the myriad blessings, both grand and minuscule, that grace your life: the innocent laughter of your child, the embrace of a peaceful night's rest, the satisfaction of a nourishing meal, the warmth of an extraordinary family, the splendor of a sunset's hues, the simple joy of clean, life-giving water, and the undeniable miracle of your very existence.

Recognizing that we already possess all we truly need, we undergo a profound transformation. We realize that we are whole and complete just as we are, and this awareness empowers us to navigate life's challenges with resilience and to nurture a sense of enduring contentment. Gratitude becomes the compass that guides us toward a life rich in abundance, appreciation, and fulfillment.

💡 Exercise: List five things in your life you are grateful for.

Challenge yourself to repeat this exercise tomorrow and every day. Read this list before you go to bed each night.

YOU ARE GOOD ENOUGH

"You are good enough. Actually, you're probably overqualified, but let's start the day off humble."
—J.R. Rim

Apply for that job even if you don't check all the boxes.
Launch that podcast even though you don't know where to begin.
Start that business you've always dreamed of.

You'll encounter enough naysayers in your life. Don't let yourself be one of them. Don't self-reject yourself from a potential opportunity just because you don't feel ready—none of us feel prepared when we start anything new.

Every expert was once a novice, every master an apprentice. Ride through the fear until it becomes routine. Just start, and with each passing day, strive to get better.

Consider this: Men are known to apply for jobs with only 60% of the qualifications, while women often wait until they meet 100% of the requirements. Be the applicant who applies for a job, knowing that even if you don't tick all the boxes, your unwavering determination, resilience, and hunger will compensate for any perceived deficiencies. This, my friend, is the true essence of being overqualified.

💡 Exercise: Unearth Your Growth Journey

This exercise aims to remind you of your inherent ability to grow and improve by reflecting on your achievements. It encourages you to confidently embrace new challenges, knowing that progress is achievable with dedication and effort.

Identify Five Skills or Abilities: In your journal, list five skills or abilities you excel at today. These could be anything, from riding a bike, cooking, playing an instrument, or even proficiency in a software program. Next to each skill, briefly describe when you started learning it and any memories associated with your initial attempts.

Reflect on Your Learning Journey: For each skill on your list, ponder the time it took for you to progress from a beginner to your current level of proficiency.

Write down your thoughts and feelings about the journey. Were there moments of frustration, challenges, or self-doubt? How did you overcome them?

Acknowledge Your Growth: Consider the significant improvements you've made in each skill. Reflect on the dedication, practice, and learning that brought you to where you are today. Write a brief note next to each skill to acknowledge your growth and accomplishments.

Apply the Lesson to New Challenges: Think about a new skill or endeavor you've been contemplating but have yet to start because you feel inexperienced or uncertain.

Set Realistic Expectations: Remember that every skill or ability you've mastered starts with a beginner's mindset. It took time and effort to progress. Acknowledge that, just like in the past, you can improve and grow with dedication, practice, and patience.

Commit to Taking the First Step: Choose a specific action or step to learn or practice a new skill or endeavor. Write down this actionable step and set a date for when you'll take it.

Embrace the Journey: Approach this new challenge with the understanding that your progress may take time, but it will be rewarding.

Keep your journal as a reminder of your past growth and resilience and use it to track your progress as you embark on this new journey.

This exercise reinforces that personal growth and skill development are ongoing processes. By reflecting on your past achievements and embracing the journey, you can confidently approach new challenges and believe improvement is possible with dedication and perseverance.

CHANGE REQUIRES CONSISTENT ACTION

Transformation Requires Consistent Action:
We Become What We Do Daily

Change Requires Consistent Action

I would craft New Year's resolutions, only to watch them quickly fizzle out. I struggled with the same 10 pounds, losing and regaining them for over a decade. Does this scenario sound all too familiar? Sure, I'd diligently follow an improvement plan for the initial week, maybe even a month if my discipline held, but I would inevitably revert to my old habits.

It wasn't until I embraced this pivotal life lesson that my transformation took hold: Meaningful change necessitates unwavering, daily action. While everyone craves instant success, substantial change emerges from the cumulative impact of small, daily decisions made over weeks, months, and years. Each choice, whether positive or negative, shapes our future selves.

My Personal Story of Change

In the case of those pesky 10 pounds, they ballooned into an extra 25 pounds during the pandemic. That might not sound significant, but when you are 5'2" tall, the difference between a dime and 25 cents becomes rather pronounced. During this period, I received my lab reports and the alarming news that I was pre-diabetic.

While my previous attempts at weight loss were mainly driven by vanity, this revelation struck a deeper chord. My father had Type 2 Diabetes, which ultimately led to kidney failure. I vividly recall being just 15 years old, learning to drive so I could transport my father to his dialysis appointments.

At that moment, I knew I didn't want to endure the suffering my father had experienced, and more profoundly, I didn't want my daughter to have to care for me because I had neglected my health. I yearned to live as long as possible to witness my daughter's walk down the aisle. I wanted to be spry enough to play with my future grandchildren and remain healthy.

Finally, I had found my "why."

And once I unearthed my "why," I was able to unearth my "how."

Amidst the pandemic, I shed over 35 pounds. Empowered by a compelling reason, I began with small steps. It commenced with a simple one-block walk, gradually evolving into covering a mile and running six miles. As I delved deeper into health, I discovered that cardio alone wouldn't suffice; I needed to incorporate weightlifting to bolster bone health and longevity. Whole foods replaced processed foods.

None of this occurred overnight. It took nearly a year to shed all the weight, and during the maintenance phase, I couldn't revert to my old habits. I had to become the person I aspired to be. My habits and daily actions were how I became that person: No longer a couch potato, I had transformed into an athlete, requiring proper fuel and a regimen befitting an athlete. The path to lasting change mandates unwavering, consistent action.

So Why Is It So Hard to Change?

Taking action on our purpose can often feel like the most challenging step. How many times have we held back due to fear or the nagging voice in the back of our head telling us we aren't enough? That we're not ready?

It's only natural to have imposter syndrome when you start something new. It's so much easier to accept the status quo, to stay stuck where we are, what we know. Our comfort zone is, well, comfortable because it's familiar territory. It's like a well-worn couch—cozy, predictable, and irresistibly tempting.

Growth is Scary

Growth is scary because it's new. It's so much easier to stay in the comfort of mediocrity. Growth requires us to traverse the unknown. It requires us to stretch ourselves. Change, quite simply, requires changing who we are. However, that's easier said than done.

But here's the deal: you've already started the path to growth by reading this book. You are already on the path to becoming your best self.

In Lesson 1, you took a crucial step by pinpointing what truly holds meaning. Lesson 2 equips you with the tools to cultivate the right mindset, setting the stage for pursuing what matters most. Lesson 3 focuses on our understanding that change requires action. It requires us to change who we are to create our best life. But first, we must believe we can. After all, if you don't believe in yourself, why take that first step, right?

Let's draw inspiration from Nora Roberts, celebrated for her romance novels and timeless wisdom: "If you don't go after what you want, you'll never have it. If you don't ask, the answer is always no. If you don't step forward, you're always in the same place."

Embrace Growth

Embracing growth and change can be scary; there's no denying that. It means venturing into the unknown, taking calculated risks, and placing a bet on yourself. It involves a willingness to learn and try new things. It means understanding that failure is not something to be feared but a natural process of learning and growing.

But here's the beautiful part: Through change and growth, we unearth our true selves, the individuals God intended us to be. It's about becoming the best version of ourselves. It's about becoming the absolute best version of ourselves, my friend!

Live a Big Life

The unknown can seem daunting, but let's not allow it to hinder our growth. You were designed for an expansive life that aligns with your unique definition of "big," even if that means embracing the simplicity of it all.

So, my friend, as you step into the uncharted territory of living your purpose, remember this: You have the courage, the wisdom, and the heart to live a life that's both big and beautiful, a life that resonates with your unique definition of "big." The world is yours for the taking!

Know this deep down: You've already got everything you need—an authentic purpose and the mindset of a champion. Now is the moment to take action, to turn those aspirations into tangible realities. You've reached a point where you're primed and ready to start living out your purpose, making meaningful strides in the real world. All that remains is to set sail to align your actions with your purpose, and I promise you, my friend, that the forthcoming lessons will be your compass on this thrilling journey!

"Let's face it, you'll never have all the answers. Just start. You can figure it out as you go. Focus on daily incremental improvements. Don't fixate on perfection–strive to improve each day. Optimize while you're in the process of building whatever it is you're creating. The answers reveal themselves in the journey, not in the waiting."

–Lan Phan

Believe in yourself.
Bet on yourself.
Trust in your God-given talents.

Deep within, you possess everything necessary to conquer your goals and live your dream life. Yes, this journey begins with persistence and an unwavering belief in yourself.

Bet on yourself. It's time you take that pivotal first step: leap if you must, and if you can't jump, crawl. Whatever your pace, just keep moving in the direction of your dreams.

The key is to start. The key is to move toward your goals. And once you've begun, never stop. Keep pushing forward relentlessly.

Remember, it is all about believing in yourself. From there, it's the decision to start and progress toward the unwavering pursuit of your dreams. So, keep moving forward. You've got this!

"Positive thinking alone is garbage. Dreams don't happen until you take daily and consistent action to make them a reality."

–Lan Phan

OUR DREAMS REQUIRE ACTION

Positive thinking is essential, but dreams don't work unless you put in the work. We manifest our desired life through our actions, compounded daily.

Take inventory of what you are doing each day.

What are you eating and consuming? Who do you choose to surround yourself with? Are you doing something each day that gets you closer to your goals? Do you prioritize self-care and extend compassion to both you and others?

Are you becoming the person who is worthy of the life you want to live?

Consider this: If you seek love, are you actively embodying love in your interactions? Are you a loving person who deserves to be loved?

If you desire health, are you committed to regular exercise and a wholesome diet?

You need to put in the work. Don't just want it. Do it. Each day, invest effort towards your goals.

Believe in your ability to manifest your ideal life by relentlessly pursuing your dreams until they become your reality.

Leave behind the doubt and become who you were made to be.

COMMIT TO CHANGE

"No one can stop you once you have decided to grow."
—Sangeeta Rana

Your life transforms when you abandon self-doubt, step out of your comfort zone, and embark on a journey of personal and professional growth.

Your path to success is closely tied to your commitment to daily, consistent personal and professional development. Success isn't just something that randomly happens to people; it's something you actively create by becoming the best version of yourself.

Let that sink in. Commit it to heart. If you want change, remember that it begins with you. So stop waiting for someone to save you. You have always been the hero in your story.

Is change a challenging journey? Undoubtedly.

But you know what's even more challenging: Staying stuck in places and relationships you've outgrown.

So don't let fear or hesitation hold you back from unlocking your full potential and embracing growth. You have everything you need to build your dream life.

💡 **Empowering Exercise:** If you desire change, you must be the change. Take a moment to reflect on the life purpose you uncovered in Lesson 1. Identify the areas and gaps you must address to start living a more purposeful and fulfilling life.

"Stop making things so complicated. Consistency. That's it. That's the message. If you want to get better at anything, do it daily."

–Lan Phan

CONSISTENCY IS KEY

Stop making things so complicated. Be consistent if you want to reach your goals and achieve your dreams. Consistency has always been the prerequisite for transformation. It's showing up day in and day out, no matter the circumstances. While it might not sound as glamorous as overnight success, the regular beat of the drum of consistency creates the foundation for lasting change.

When you embark on a transformation journey, you rewire your habits, beliefs, and mindset. Consistency is the glue and bridge to achieving your goals and dreams. It is the compass guiding you through the ups and downs. It's the force that propels you forward when your motivation is waning, and the obstacles seem insurmountable.

Consistency is the chisel that sculpts your future; Every day, you chip away at your old self, revealing the potential within. It's about doing the right things, even when it's hard. Over time, these daily actions accumulate, creating a compound effect that leads to transformation.

Moreover, consistency instills trust - trust in yourself and those around you. As you follow through on your commitments, even when no one is watching, you reinforce the belief that change is possible. This self-trust becomes the bedrock of your transformation. It silences the inner critic and fuels you to new heights.

Ultimately, consistency is the bridge that connects who you are today to who you aspire to become. It's the force that turns intentions into reality dreams into achievements. So, as you embark on your transformation journey, remember that while the path may be long and challenging, your unwavering consistency will lead you to the transformation you seek.

DECIDE TO GROW

"To attract better, you have to become better. You can't do the same things and expect change. Transform your mindset. Upgrade your habits. Think positive. Be hopeful and consistent with your evolution. It all starts with you and how you feel about yourself."
—Idil Ahmed

It always starts with you.
It begins with finding a reason and purpose that lights the fire within you. If your why is big enough, you'll find your how.

Upgrade your mindset. Your mind is the master key to your destiny. Upgrade it, and you'll unlock doors you never even knew existed.

Upgrade your skill set. Sharpen those tools in your arsenal. Mastery is a journey, and each step forward matters. Work on getting better each day.

Upgrade your habits. Your habits are the rudder steering the ship of your life. Let go of negative habits holding you back and focus on creating positive ones that propel you forward.

Upgrade who you spend time with. If we are the average of who we spend the most time with, let us choose wisely. Elevate your tribe. Surround yourself with those who inspire and challenge you to reach higher.

Change starts with changing who we are. You're not stuck; you're just holding on to the past, the status quo. Let that shit go. It's time to break free.

Choose growth. Let go of what no longer serves you. Make a conscious decision to evolve and watch as your world transforms before your very eyes.

💡 Exercise: Crafting Daily Habits for Transformation

In this exercise, you will identify five daily habits that will propel you toward becoming your ideal self.

1. Mindset Mastery: Begin by reflecting on your current mindset. What beliefs or thought patterns are holding you back? Write down at least one limiting belief that you're aware of. Now, envision your ideal self. What empowering ideas and thoughts does this version of you possess? Write down one or more positive affirmations or beliefs that align with your ideal self.

   Daily Habit: Every morning, spend 5-10 minutes in quiet reflection, repeating your chosen affirmations or empowering beliefs to shift your mindset toward your ideal self.

2. Skill Development: Consider the skills or abilities that bring you closer to your ideal self. It could be related to your career, personal growth, or a hobby.

   Daily Habit: Dedicate 30 minutes each day to skill development. This could involve reading, practicing, or learning something new that aligns with your goals.

3. Habit Refinement: Identify a habit you currently have that doesn't serve your progress toward your ideal self. It could be procrastination, excessive screen time, or unhealthy eating.

   Daily Habit: Focus on breaking this harmful habit by replacing it with a positive one. For example, if you're prone to procrastination, allocate 10 minutes daily to work on a task you've been avoiding.

4. Positive Influences: Consider the people you spend the most time with. Are they supportive and aligned with your goals, or do they hold you back?

Daily Habit: Make a conscious effort to spend time with individuals who inspire and encourage your growth. Reach out to one such person daily, whether a mentor, friend, or colleague, and engage in a meaningful conversation.

5. Daily Reflection: Regular reflection ensures you stay on track toward your ideal self.

    Daily Habit: Dedicate 10-15 minutes before bedtime for reflection. Ask yourself: "What did I do today that brought me closer to my ideal self?" and "What could I have done better?" Use these insights to adjust your habits and actions for the next day.

Remember, the consistency of these daily habits will gradually lead you toward becoming your ideal self. Stay committed and watch your transformation unfold.

BE A BEGINNER

"Be Brave Enough to Suck at Something New."
—Jon Acuff

Every expert started as a beginner. You must start somewhere. Right?

Be okay with being terrible in the beginning. Be okay with being mediocre in the middle. And if you're having fun, be OK with whatever level you're at in the process.

The key is maintaining a beginner's mindset throughout your life; that's where the true victory lies.

Sometimes, the win is conquering your fears.
Sometimes, the win is learning something new.
Sometimes, the win is stretching your comfort zone to its limit.
Sometimes, the win is making friends along the way.
Sometimes, the win is laughing at yourself.
Sometimes, the win is joy.
Sometimes, the win is learning that you don't like what you just tried!

Embrace it all!
Remember that the journey and growth along the way matter most. Enjoy every moment along the way and embrace all that comes your way.

💡 Exercise: Embrace Your Fears

Purpose: This exercise encourages you to explore the activities or experiences you'd pursue if the fear of failure or judgment didn't hold you back.

- Take a moment to contemplate what you would wholeheartedly try if you weren't afraid of failure, ridicule, or judgment. Consider various activities or experiences that pique your interest but have remained untouched due to fear. These could include dancing, singing, learning a new language, or anything else you've yet to try.

- Reflect on a personal example from your life. For me personally, my biggest fear for years was karaoke. Seriously. Describe an instance where you let go of your inhibitions and fear to dive headfirst into something you once found intimidating.
- Now, challenge yourself to confront one of your fears. Choose one of the activities or experiences you identified in Step 1 and commit to trying it, even if it terrifies you.
- As you face your fear and engage in the chosen activity, pay close attention to how your perception changes. Document your feelings, thoughts, and experiences as you venture into this fear-ridden territory.
- After the experience, reflect on what you've learned. How did confronting your fear affect your perception of it? Did it prove to be less daunting than anticipated?

Following these steps, you'll identify your fearless desires and embark on a journey to conquer your fears and expand your horizons. Remember that facing your fears can lead to newfound confidence and a broader perspective on what you can achieve.

JUST START

Start Now.
Start Where You Are.
Start with fear.
Start with pain.
Start with doubt.
Start with hands shaking.
Start with voice trembling.
Just Start.
—Ijeoma Umebinyuo

Taking that first step on a new journey has always been the most formidable hurdle to overcome. All our doubts and insecurities converge at that very starting point. We stand on the precipice, hesitating, pausing, allowing the shadow of doubt to cast its veil over our minds.

Yet here's the remarkable part: Once that initial step is taken, a transformation begins. With each subsequent stride, our confidence swells, and we cultivate the muscle memory of progress. It becomes second nature, like breathing.

Consider this: Would we ever scold babies for stumbling on their first step? No, because we understand that it's in getting back up that the muscles are forged, and resilience is born. It's an essential part of building strength.

So why, then, are we so relentless in our self-critique?

It's time to shatter that self-imposed barrier. Seize that inaugural step with unwavering resolve, for it is the key that unlocks the door to your journey of growth and self-discovery. Take that first step already. What are you waiting for?

💡 Exercise: What's one thing you've wanted to do but haven't started yet?

Today, let's initiate that dream with a small yet powerful step.

If, for instance, your goal is to master a new language, commence your journey by committing to memorize a single word today.

Here's Your Daily Ritual:

- Start with One: Begin with a single word. Learn it, embrace it, and make it your own.
- Consistency is Key: Promise yourself to memorize one new word every day. Relish the process; let it become a part of your daily routine.
- Progressive Growth: Go beyond just one word as you gain confidence and proficiency. Add progressively larger goals, building your vocabulary and fluency.

This seemingly modest step today is the spark that ignites the fire of your ambition. By committing to this daily ritual, you'll watch your goals come to life, one word at a time.

"One-hundred fifty thousand people in the world did not wake up this morning. Strive to live the life you want, starting today. Tomorrow is not promised. Stop dwelling on the past or worrying about the future. The only reality that truly matters is this very moment. Don't squander the gift you've been given, for life is a precious gift. Embrace it, seize it, and make it your own. What are you waiting for? There has never been a more perfect time than today."

–Lan Phan

DO IT NOW

"One day you will wake up, and there won't be any more time to do the things you've always wanted. Do it now."
—*Paulo Coelho*

This universal truth applies to us all: The day will come when you've exhausted your chances to pursue your long-held desires. Don't wait to start living. Chase your dreams till they become reality.

When we are young, we think we have all the time in the world, but time is a fleeting journey. On average, we're granted just 27,375 days.

Make each of those days count.

What are you waiting for?
Now is the time to find happiness.
Now is the time to invest in yourself.
Now is the time to express your love for those around you.
Now is the time to finally take that vacation with your family.
Now is the time to pursue your dreams.

Stop waiting. The right time has always been now.

💡 Exercise: Crafting Your Legacy

Close your eyes and envision a scene at your funeral. As you observe, imagine your friends, family, and colleagues taking turns to share their eulogies, painting a picture of your life.

Your Journal Reflective Session:

For the next 10 minutes, let your thoughts flow freely as you consider these questions:

- Friends: What would you want your friends to say about you? What qualities, memories, and impacts would you hope they highlight?

- Family: Imagine the words of your family members. What kind of loving and memorable stories would you like them to recall?
- Colleagues: Think about your professional life. What accomplishments and traits would you wish your colleagues to recognize and celebrate?

As you delve into these reflections, consider whether you feel content with the life you've lived thus far or if there are aspects where you wish you had done more. Use this exercise as a compass for aligning your actions with your values and aspirations, ensuring that your life story is one you're proud to leave behind.

WRITE YOUR DREAMS DOWN

"Writing your goals down in your journal sends a signal
to your brain that says: "This is important to me."
—Unknown

Do you want to manifest your dreams?

Let me tell you how. How many of you have taken the time to put your dreams and aspirations on paper? Few things can enhance your intentionality as effectively as daily journaling. The act of putting pen to paper holds immense power.

Why, may you ask? Research indicates that you are 42 percent more likely to achieve your goals when you write them down.

We don't only realize our dreams through hope; action plays a crucial role, too. Putting your goals in writing is a potent tool for clarifying the steps needed to achieve them.

💡 **Exercise: Take a moment to pause and reflect on the possibilities that could unfold if you allowed yourself to dream without limits.**

Envision your professional and personal life as if every dream you ever had come to fruition. Now, grab your journal or a notebook and begin to bring this vision to life through words.

As you immerse yourself in this dream life, picture yourself taking incremental, actionable steps toward your goals. Visualize the determination and resilience with which you overcome obstacles and challenges. Remember that writing down your dreams and aspirations marks the essential first step toward turning them into reality.

IT'S NOT TOO LATE

"For what it's worth:
I was 43 when I got a Ph.D.
I was 51 when I started my dream job.
I was 54 when I married the love of my life.
I was 55 when I ran my first marathon.
I was 67 when I self-published my first book.
I turn 70 next year, and I can't wait."
—Douglas Lumsden

Listen to me. It's not too late. Stop saying you're too old to figure out what you want. Stop with that nonsense.

It's not your age that's limiting you. It's your limiting beliefs that have taken root. It's the relentless messages from society and the media, pushing anti-aging products, flashy cars, and quick fixes.

Imagine what would happen if you stopped caring about your age. Entire industries would crumble, and that's the truth. There are people and businesses who profit from your pain and insecurities. Read that again.

It's not too late to launch a business.
It's not too late to discover love.
It's not too late to conquer a marathon.
It's not too late to embark on adventures.
It's not too late to uncover your purpose.

Start living. Quit the futile quest to prove yourself to others. Regardless of your age, whether it's youthful or seasoned, the only limitation you face is the belief system you carry.

Ray Kroc entered the McDonald's franchise when he was 53. Nelson Mandela assumed the presidency of South Africa in 76. Julia Child hosted her first TV show at 50. It's never too late or too early to start chasing your dreams.

So, for heaven's sake, just start!

💡 Exercise: Rekindling Joy from Your Youth

Purpose: This exercise encourages you to revisit the youthful energy and enthusiasm you once had and find ways to incorporate elements of that joy into your current life.

- Close Your Eyes and Reflect: Close your eyes and begin to imagine yourself at a younger age, whether as a toddler, a teenager, or in your early twenties. Visualize the vibrant energy and enthusiasm that characterized that time in your life.
- Recall Past Passions: Think back to the activities or hobbies that brought you immense joy during that period. These could be anything from dancing, playing a sport, painting, or any other passion you have. Reflect on the specific moments of happiness they brought you.
- Rediscover Your Interests: Now, consider how you can reintegrate elements of those joyful activities into your current life. Create a list of activities or interests you want to explore or rediscover.
- Choose One Activity: From your list, select one activity or interest that resonates with you the most. Commit to engage in this chosen activity within the next week. This commitment is a concrete step toward rekindling the joy of your youth.
- Embrace the Timeless Joy: Remember that age is merely a number; you can tap into joy at any stage of life. Keep this exercise as a gentle reminder that you can always reconnect with the happiness you once experienced.

Following these steps reignite the spark of joy from your younger days and take tangible steps to incorporate it into your current life, affirming that joy knows no age boundaries.

BET ON YOURSELF

"I don't gamble. But if there's one thing I'm willing to bet on, it's myself."
—Beyonce

You're making a powerful proclamation when you finally decide to start betting on yourself. It's a declaration of your self-worth and a testament to your belief in your untapped potential and cherished dreams.

By investing in yourself, you open the door to significant victories. You permit yourself to pursue those dreams waiting in the wings. And even though you may not capture every dream in your grasp, you inch closer with every stride, bringing your aspirations closer to reality.

In the beginning, betting on yourself might seem like trivial steps. Some days, the mere act of rising from your bed becomes a bold statement of defiance.

When you bet on yourself, you're wagering on your unwavering resilience, unrelenting hustle, burning passion, and the boundless potential within you. It's a bet on your capacity to shape your destiny and turn your dreams into reality.

💡 Exercise: Take an inventory of your life.

Are you taking chances on yourself by going after opportunities and stretch goals? Or are you letting them pass because you're afraid of failure?

Ask yourself, 'What's the worst thing that could happen if you bet on yourself?' Then, if the worst-case scenario is manageable, create an action plan that will get you closer to your dreams.

INVEST YOUR TIME WISELY

"Your time is limited, so don't waste it living someone else's life. Don't be trapped by dogma—which is living with the results of other people's thinking."
—Steve Jobs

If we are fortunate, we get 4,732 weeks to live. Our most treasured possessions are neither wealth nor material possessions but our time and energy. Unfortunately, many of us fritter away these invaluable resources on inconsequential pursuits and superficial relationships.

We squander this finite commodity as we mindlessly scroll through social media, consumed by mind-numbing reality shows, all the while living vicariously through the lives of people we have never met. Regrettably, those who genuinely care for us and whom we hold dear are left with the remainder of our dwindling attention span.

These time drains squander our precious hours and lead us astray from our genuine purpose. Instead of wholeheartedly committing to building our empires, nurturing authentic relationships, and unflinchingly pursuing our dreams, we often become trapped in trivial distractions.

What if, instead of squandering our time, we focused on:

Nourishing our bodies
Fueling our health
Chasing our dreams
Creating lasting and loving relationships
Being of service to others
Learning and growing each day
Leaving the world better than we found it.

Time is the currency of our life; don't waste it on things that will bankrupt you. Instead, invest each moment in the pursuit of your best life. We are allotted a mere 4,732 weeks in this world; treat each second as your most precious possession—because it is."

💡 Exercise: Time Investment Reflection

Reflect on how you spend your time on a typical day or week. Think about activities that make you laugh, contribute to your financial well-being, allow you to connect with loved ones, or provide you with rest.

Write down at least three activities or areas where you believe your time is well-invested and positively contributes to your life. Next, jot down any activities or habits you consider time-wasting or draining.

Finally, commit to adjusting your daily or weekly schedule to prioritize the activities that align with your life goals and values. Consider optimizing your time and energy to live your best life each day.

EMBRACE MISTAKES

"The only man who never makes mistakes is
the man who never does anything."
—Theodore Roosevelt

Congratulations are in order!
You've encountered setbacks, missed the mark, and made mistakes. You deserve a round of applause!

The highest form of failure is inaction. Your stumbles and errors signify that you've dared to step into the arena of life. You've risen each morning, laced up your boots, and dedicated yourself to chasing your dreams.

Success, my friend, is a numbers game. The more effort you invest in yourself and your pursuits, the greater your chances of success. Stumbling is inevitable; it's an integral part of the journey. Our growth stems more from the lessons we glean from our mistakes than our effortless triumphs.

In our society, we often spotlight the "success stories": the grand IPOs, the accolades, the polished LinkedIn profiles boasting new titles. What remains concealed are the countless hours of relentless effort, the rejection, and the naysayers trying to pull us down.

Change the lens through which you view the world, and the world will change in response. Alter your mindset, and you have the power to shape your destiny.

💡 Exercise: Shattering the Shame-Failure Link

Many of us were conditioned to link shame with failure in our upbringing. But what if we flipped the script and celebrated loss as the essential steppingstone to victory? Take inspiration from Sara Blakely, the visionary founder of Spanx, who shared a family tradition of recounting daily failures during dinner. In her household, failure was not shamed; it was celebrated.

Imagine a life where we fearlessly embrace failure, recognizing it as an integral part of our path to growth. The next time you stumble and falter, I encourage you to applaud yourself. Why? Because stumbling signifies that you dared to try. It means that you're in the process of learning and evolving. Celebrate those stumbles as they pave the way for your ultimate success.

DON'T LET FEAR STOP YOU

> *"Courage doesn't mean you don't get afraid. Courage means you don't let fear stop you."*
> *—Bethany Hamilton*

Sticking to the status quo and clinging to detrimental habits, relationships, and unfulfilling jobs is often the path of least resistance. We say we want change, but our actions don't align with our words. Regrettably, we either give up or never take the first step toward change.

Yes, change is scary. Do it anyway. More often than not, our fears are not grounded in reality. A study by the Department of Psychology at the University of Pennsylvania revealed that 91 percent of our worries never come to pass.

Fear is akin to a rocking chair—it's something to occupy your time with but won't propel you toward any real destination. So, whatever you've been longing to pursue, take that leap. That worst-case scenario probably won't happen, so why worry?

Exercise: Take the First Step Toward Progress

Think about a project, goal, or aspiration you've been holding back due to doubt, fear, or overthinking. It could be something as significant as a career change or as simple as a creative project.

Identify Your Hesitations: In writing, list the doubts and fears that have prevented you from taking the first step toward this goal. Ask yourself, "What's the worst that can happen?" Sometimes, by directly addressing the worst-case scenario, we can disarm the fear tied to the uncertainty.

For each doubt or fear you've listed, challenge yourself to reframe it more positively or freely. Consider how acting can lead to growth and learning, even if mistakes occur. Ask yourself if you can overcome the worst-case scenario.

Break down your goal into smaller, manageable steps. Start with the very first step, no matter how minor.

Take that initial step within a specific timeframe. Hold yourself accountable.

After taking that first step, reflect on your experience. What did you learn? How did it feel to overcome that initial hurdle? Use this reflection to adjust your action plan and keep moving forward.

This exercise encourages you to confront your hesitations and move beyond overthinking by taking concrete action.

GET UP!

*"Inaction breeds doubt and fear. Action breeds confidence
and courage. If you want to conquer fear, do not sit at
home and think about it. Go out and get busy."*
–Dale Carnegie

Don't let fear hold you back. Do it scared. Confront fear head-on and press forward. That's the only antidote to fear. Action. To start living, you must rise, venture out, and take decisive action. Fortune rewards the bold.

Small, manageable steps are the most effective strategy to overcome your fears and surmount challenges. With each stride, you will progress so far from your once-formidable fears that they no longer have power over you.

Believe in yourself—you've got this. Let's embark on this journey with unwavering faith and determination!

💡 Exercise: How Do You Devour an Elephant? One Bite at a Time

Take a substantial goal you're eager to achieve and deconstruct it into smaller, manageable pieces and milestones. Then, go even further by breaking those pieces into smaller, digestible portions.

Instead of fixating on the grand objective, channel your energy into celebrating each small milestone as a significant victory. By acknowledging and rejoicing in these incremental wins, you nurture your confidence.

Remember, life is a marathon, not a sprint, and each step forward, no matter how small, propels you toward your ultimate destination.

DO THE IMPOSSIBLE

"Most of the important things in the world have been accomplished by people who have kept trying when there seemed to be no hope at all."
—Dale Carnegie

Change doesn't grow from complacency or emerge for those paralyzed by fear. It certainly won't happen for those who don't even try.

The world bends for those who persevere in the darkest hours. It transforms for those who refuse to surrender when everyone else throws in the towel and shifts when individuals unite, raising their voices to demand change.

Keep moving forward. Hold on to hope. Be the guiding light in the darkness.

Renowned psychologist and hope researcher Charles Snyder beautifully articulated, "A rainbow is a prism that sends shards of multicolored light in various directions. It lifts our spirits and makes us think of what is possible. Hope is the same—a personal rainbow of the mind."

Where there is hope, a path emerges. When we couple hope with action, we make it possible for transformation to happen.

Hopeful individuals don't idly wait for circumstances to favor them. Instead, they combine imagination with relentless action. They set clear objectives and construct precise action plans. They have unwavering faith in their abilities and potential to attain their goals. They recognize that obstacles and failures are intrinsic to the journey and adapt when faced with setbacks. These challenges don't deter them; they intensify their determination to achieve their objectives.

Where there is hope, there is always a way.

💡 Exercise: Crafting an Action-Plan for Your Aspirations

Take a moment to reflect on a dream or goal you've laid dormant. What is holding you back? Write down these fears or concerns in your journal.

Now, channel your inner resilience and hope. Imagine a rainbow of possibilities shining brightly in your mind. Envision the path toward your goal illuminated by this rainbow.

Set clear objectives for your dream or goal. What steps can you take to move closer to it? Write down these action steps in your journal.

Recognize that obstacles and setbacks are a natural part of any journey. How can you adapt and persevere when faced with challenges? Write down your strategies for overcoming obstacles.

Commit to taking the first step toward your dream or goal today. Remember, where there is hope, there is a way. Write a brief journal entry describing the action you will take to move forward, no matter how small.

Regularly revisit your journal entry to reaffirm your hope, track your progress, and stay motivated on your journey toward change and transformation.

CHALLENGE YOUR HABITS

"Get into the habit of asking yourself: Does this
support the life I'm trying to create?"
—Torey C. Richards

Our lives are the result of the countless decisions we make daily. Yet more often than not, we operate on autopilot, navigating life without intentionality, often spending time with those who may not support our desired path. If you're trying to uncover your purpose, breaking free from this autopilot mode is essential.

A pivotal starting point in this journey is clarifying your core values. These values are the bedrock of your beliefs and principles, shaping your personal and professional conduct. If you still need to identify your core values, consider revisiting Lesson 1.

Once your core values are firmly established, the key is to live by them. They become your guiding North Star, influencing every choice you make, regardless of its magnitude.

With your core values as your anchor, the question, "Does this support the life I'm trying to create?" becomes a transformative guide. Another inquiry, "Does this align with my core values and the person I aspire to become?" holds equal importance. These simple yet profound questions will clarify your decision-making and steer you toward discovering your purpose.

💡 Exercise: Take a Moment to Jot Down Ten Daily Habits or Routines

For each one, delve into a deeper introspection by asking yourself: "Does this align with my core values and the individual I aspire to become?"

Following this introspection, take proactive steps to recalibrate your daily life. Embrace more actions that draw you nearer to your core values and the person you strive to be while eliminating those activities that steer you away from the alignment you seek with your values and your envisioned self.

This exercise serves as a compass to navigate your daily life with greater intentionality, ensuring that your actions are harmonious with your deepest beliefs and aspirations.

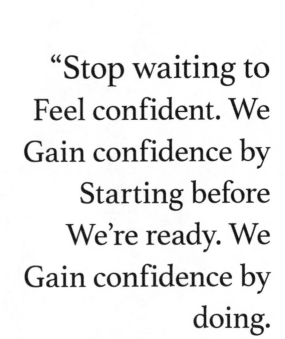

"Stop waiting to Feel confident. We Gain confidence by Starting before We're ready. We Gain confidence by doing.

–Lan Phan

STOP WAITING TO FEEL CONFIDENT

What is one of life's most tragic ironies?

Most of us wait for confidence before we start. The truth is that we gain confidence by doing. We gain confidence by starting before we are ready.

Confidence is not a prerequisite but a byproduct of doing and becoming.

That inner critic in your head screaming, "You can't do it! You're not ready. Who do you think you are?" gets silenced by doing. It gets silenced by becoming.

We become by doing.

We aren't born confident. We earn confidence by doing and becoming.

Start.
Start scared.
Start with your hands trembling.

This is how our hands become steady.
This is how we become.

SEIZE EVERY MOMENT OF LIFE'S RICHNESS

"Time is more valuable than money.
You can get more money, but you cannot get more time."
—Jim Rohn

As we rise each day, let's begin with profound gratitude. Let's approach every moment with the awareness that it could be our last. Time is our most treasured possession, the very essence of our existence. Without it, all else pales.

Armed with this profound understanding, embrace life with unbridled enthusiasm and intention.

- Embrace your children with warm hugs, for there may never be a better moment.
- Reach out to your friends and engage in meaningful conversations. Don't postpone the connection.
- Dance like no one's watching and let the joy of movement flow through you.
- Let laughter bubble forth, unburdened by restraint.

We often wait for that elusive "perfect time" to pursue our dreams. Let us abandon this notion. The life you desire is meant to be lived now, in the present moment.

💡 Exercise: Express Your Love and Appreciation

Take action today to demonstrate your love and appreciation for someone dear to you:

- Share a big bear hug with someone you love. Hold your partner's hand.
- Reach out and arrange a coffee meetup with that friend you haven't seen in forever.

- Send an appreciation text to a distant colleague, expressing your deep appreciation for their contributions and presence in your life.

Small gestures of kindness and connection can brighten someone's day and strengthen your bonds with those who matter most to you.

"Give yourself a
fighting chance to win.
Just ask already.
What's the worst that
could happen?
You might get a 'no,'
but by doing so,
you open the door
to the possibility of a 'yes.'
We create our fortune
by advocating
for ourselves."

–Lan Phan

DEMAND WHAT YOU DESERVE

I poured my heart and soul into my work, tirelessly outperforming those around me. I patiently bided my time, expecting recognition and opportunities to come my way. I waited my turn, believing my dedication would inevitably be acknowledged. However, too often, it wasn't.

Why? Because I didn't speak up. I failed to voice my contributions and aspirations. I naively assumed that my hard work would naturally catch the eye of management.

My reluctance to ask stemmed from a fear of rejection, the dread of receiving a "no."

But with age came a valuable revelation: If you don't ask, the answer will forever remain "no." So, ask boldly. By actively seeking what you desire, you exponentially increase your chances of achieving it. Don't prematurely exclude yourself from an opportunity due to the fear of rejection.

And if you still encounter a "no," remember: You possess the power to build your table, to create opportunities where none exist.

GET IT DONE!

"An idea without action is like a bow without an arrow."
–Martin Luther King

Your words may articulate your aspirations, but your actions breathe life into them. Dreams and visions are inspiring but require deliberate steps to become reality.

In corporate terminology, companies call it having a "bias toward action." I simply call it "getting shit done."

Merely wishing and hoping won't transform your dreams into reality. It won't start businesses or create fortunes.

Happiness and success have always required intentional choice and deliberate action.

To paraphrase Mahatma Gandhi, you must be the driving force for the "change you wish to see in the world" as you hold the power to shape your destiny. You are the architect of your life. So, let's take action and turn those dreams into reality.

Or as my Texan friends might say, "Let's getter done!"

💡 Exercise: The Power of the Five-Second Rule

Mel Robbins's Five-Second Rule operates on a simple yet potent premise. When your instinct nudges you to act, you have a mere five seconds to initiate a physical response, or your brain will sabotage the impulse.

Let's put this principle into practice right now. Identify one small action you've been meaning to take today. Now, together, let's count down 5-4-3-2-1, and without hesitation, take that step.

Please explore her insights further if you're intrigued by Mel Robbins's transformative methods. You can delve into her wisdom through her enlightening YouTube content or book, "The 5 Second Rule."

YOU ARE WORTHY

"You are worthy now. Not when you get that job, not when you lose 20 pounds, not when people know who you are. Now. Simply because you exist."
—Nina Parker

You don't need other people's approval to validate your worthiness; you are inherently worthy just as you are.

Let's be clear: There's nothing wrong with aspiring to improve, strive for excellence, or make meaningful contributions to the world. However, what's essential to recognize is that throughout our lives, we often chase after titles and shiny objects, believing they will bestow a sense of worthiness upon us.

In truth, love and happiness have always been our birthright, available to us from the outset.

True worthiness is rooted in self-love, embracing yourself with all your imperfections, and acknowledging that you deserve the best life offers.

Many of us delay our sense of worthiness, waiting for an imaginary finish line that seems to recede the closer we draw to it. The paradox of life lies in the fact that genuine transformation occurs when we wholeheartedly love and accept ourselves just as we are.

While you embark on the journey of self-improvement, always remember to extend love and kindness to yourself along the way

💡 Exercise: Write a Love Letter to Yourself

Purpose: This exercise aims to boost your self-esteem and self-love by writing a letter to yourself, highlighting the qualities you admire most.

Begin by writing a heartfelt love letter to yourself. In this letter, focus on what you love most about yourself. You can use the following structure as a guide:

- Start with an opening, such as "Dear [Your Name],"
- Share the qualities you genuinely love and appreciate about yourself. These can range from personality traits to experiences or actions demonstrating your character. For instance, if you admire your loyalty, express it with specific examples like those in the example.

Challenge yourself to list at least 10 qualities, attributes, or experiences you hold dear about yourself. Include a mix of both significant and minor aspects that contribute to your self-esteem.

Conclude your letter with words of self-affirmation and encouragement. Mention how reading this letter can serve as a source of motivation and a reminder of your unique worth.

Save this letter in a safe and easily accessible place. Reread this letter whenever you need a confidence boost or a reminder of your self-worth. Make it a habit to revisit it often.

This exercise serves as a powerful tool for nurturing self-love and self-appreciation. It helps you recognize and celebrate your unique qualities and experiences, reinforcing a positive self-image.

"You're creating problems in your head again. Stop that."

–Lan Phan

STOP OVERTHINKING

Stop waiting for permission. Stop waiting for someone to choose you.

Just do it.
Start already.
Do it afraid.

That fear in your belly won't go away until you face that challenge you've wanted to tackle for so long.

You won't get better till you start, stumble, and get back up again. Again. And again.

You will make mistakes. That's a given. However, falling and getting back up is how you get better. There is no perfect route to success. There just isn't.

Stop waiting for perfection when progress is what you need. But you can't progress when you're too busy thinking about what can go wrong. Success requires thought coupled with action and sealed with faith.

You've been ready. The time has always been now. Take the first step and keep improving, one step at a time. It gets easier once you let go of the doubt and take that first step.

REST

"You don't need to be busy. You don't need to justify your existence in terms of productivity. Rest is an essential part of survival. An essential part of us."
—Matt Haig

It's time to reimagine the concept of productivity.
Resting is doing.
Silence is doing.
Meditation is doing.
Being in nature is doing.
Self-care is doing.

Just as you wouldn't dismiss refueling your car as inconsequential, why should you trivialize the care and restoration of your health and well-being?

💡 Exercise: Conduct a Holistic Wellness Assessment

It's time for a comprehensive evaluation of your overall well-being. Take a moment to reflect on the following aspects:

- Sleep: How many hours of sleep are you getting each night? Is it enough to rejuvenate your body and mind?
- Rest and Recharge: Do you allow yourself the necessary downtime to rest and recharge physically and mentally?
- Sun Exposure: Are you spending time outdoors, basking in the sun's natural energy, or are you confined indoors for extended periods?
- Physical Activity: Are you sedentary, glued to your office chair, or actively engaging in physical activities?

Once you've completed your wellness audit, identify at least three actionable steps to enhance your overall well-being.

For example, if you're struggling with sleep, establish a calming nighttime routine or aim to get to bed 10 minutes earlier each night. Consider leaving your cell phone in another room to minimize distractions.

Small, intentional adjustments in these areas can profoundly impact your holistic wellness.

"Being kind
doesn't come with a price
tag, but it's the most valuable
thing you can give anyone."

–Lan Phan

KINDNESS AS A KEY TO SUCCESS

The Carnegie Institute of Technology research reveals that 85 percent of your financial achievements can be attributed to your personality and capacity to communicate, negotiate, and lead. Surprisingly, only 15 percent is linked to your technical knowledge.

This insight sheds light on the undeniable potency of kindness, a quality that embodies a virtuous character and wields considerable influence in business. Those who lead with compassion tend to excel in various facets of their professional lives. They cultivate stronger relationships, become adept networkers, excel in salesmanship, and prove themselves influential leaders and team members.

What spontaneous act of kindness can you undertake right now? It could be as simple as calling a friend to convey your heartfelt appreciation or as glorious as your creativity permits.

Upon completing this act of kindness, take a moment to think about the emotions it stirred within you. Always remember that, especially when confronted with adversity. Kindness possesses a remarkable transformative power that can profoundly impact your journey toward success.

BE SILLY

"Have fun. Success will follow.
If you aren't having fun, you are doing it wrong."
—Richard Branson

When was the last time you jumped into a muddy puddle?

Stop being so serious. Have fun. Laugh a little. Let loose and allow yourself to laugh freely. Remember, most people are too engrossed in their worlds to notice what you're doing.

So go ahead, unleash your inner goofball. Giggle until your belly aches.

In the workplace, fostering an environment where laughter reverberates in the hallways is essential for nurturing a positive culture and retaining your team members.

Building a vibrant workplace culture plays a pivotal role in employee engagement. According to a Gallup study, engaged employees are 50 percent less likely to seek new job opportunities.

💡 Exercise: Laugh Audit

When did you last share a belly laugh that made your stomachache from uncontrollable mirth? If it feels like ages, it's time to intentionally carve out moments for amusement and laughter.

Reach out to that friend who always brings a smile to your face.
Spend quality time playing with your children.
Indulge in a hilarious movie or comedy show.

Remember, it's crucial to prioritize fun and play alongside your responsibilities and work commitments.

LIFT OTHERS

"We rise by lifting others."
—Robert Ingersoll

Keep sight of the profound truth that our ascent is intrinsically tied to uplifting others. Extending your hand in volunteer work, contributing resources, or dedicating your energy to aid those in need isn't merely a gift to the world; it's a transformative experience for yourself. Numerous studies affirm that helping others remarkably impacts your happiness, health, and overall well-being.

Here are some compelling benefits:

- Enhances Longevity: Altruism has been linked to a longer and more fulfilling life.
- Spreads Altruism: Acts of kindness and generosity tend to inspire others, creating a ripple effect of benevolence.
- Elevates Happiness: Assisting others is a potent source of personal happiness and contentment.
- Pain Alleviation: Helping others has been known to mitigate chronic pain and discomfort.
- Reduces Blood Pressure: Engaging in altruistic acts can lower blood pressure, promoting cardiovascular health.
- Fulfills a Sense of Purpose: Helping others imparts a profound sense of purpose and satisfaction.

In essence, the lesson is clear: When we uplift others, we simultaneously elevate ourselves.

💡 Exercise: Take Action: Volunteer and Build Community Connections

Suppose you've found yourself delaying your involvement in volunteering or community outreach. In that case, it's time to identify a project or community service endeavor that aligns with your interests and schedule it throughout the year. This is a powerful way to extend your assistance to others and a fantastic avenue for nurturing friendships and forging meaningful connections within your community.

BUILD DAILY HABITS FOR SUCCESS

"Success doesn't come from what you do occasionally.
But what you do consistently."
—Marie Forleo

Take a moment to reflect on your daily routines and habits.

What do you find yourself doing day in and day out?
What internal dialogues or self-talk patterns do you engage in, and are they empowering or limiting?

Success isn't a random occurrence; it results from our daily choices.

All these elements contribute to our journey toward success, from our dietary preferences to our clothing choices, the company we keep, the literature we consume, our inner self-talk, and the effort we invest.

If you aim for success, channel your focus into your daily actions and habits.

💡 Exercise: Evaluate Your Daily Habits for Alignment with Your Goals

Take a moment to list 10 daily activities that make up your routine. Pay close attention to your habits as they shape your life. Once you've compiled your list, assess which practices propel you toward your purpose and are in harmony with your core values.

Now, consider which actions might steer you away from your desired objectives. For instance, if you prioritize health as a core value but find yourself smoking, there must be more alignment. It's crucial to recognize these inconsistencies and work toward reducing negative habits while introducing positive ones that align with your goals.

Strive for daily and consistent practices that propel you toward the life you envision.

LEARN TO PRIORITIZE

"You can have everything you want, just not all at once."
—Oprah

I frequently advise busy executives to make change more manageable by incorporating micro-improvements or small daily habits into their routines. The typical response I receive from these busy individuals, whether they are executives or founders, is consistent: "I don't have the time."

In return, I ask: "Did you have time to brush your teeth this morning?" If yes, I counter, "I thought you didn't have time?" We have time for the things we prioritize in our lives. You have time; you have yet to make it a priority. That's a significant distinction.

Ironically, we often deprioritize the things that matter the most: our health, our family, our social connections, and even having fun. We put "urgent" matters ahead of what's essential—for instance, responding to your demanding boss's 4 a.m. emails or volunteering to chair the PTA bakeoff out of guilt.

I'm about to reveal a life-changing secret embodied in a single word:

Ready?

Seriously, are you prepared?

Hint: It starts with an "N" and ends with an "O."
Have you guessed it yet?
The magical word is "NO."

Learn to say "no" more often, enabling you to say "yes" to the things that genuinely matter.

If you're feeling overwhelmed or burnt out, it's likely because you're saying "yes" to the wrong things or agreeing to too many good things with tight deadlines. Embrace the power of "no," and don't hesitate to ask for assistance when needed.

💡 Exercise: Explore the Eisenhower Matrix

Take the time to familiarize yourself with the Eisenhower Matrix, a valuable decision-making tool designed to assist you in distinguishing between important, unimportant, and non-urgent tasks. This matrix organizes your tasks into four distinct boxes, enabling you to effectively prioritize what requires immediate attention and what can be deferred. Recognizing what holds the highest significance is a critical component of leading a purposeful life.

DO WHAT SCARES YOU

"I am learning every day to allow the space between where I want to be and where I am to inspire me and not terrify me."
—Tracy Ellis

Growth is scary.
It means taking risks.
It means betting on yourself.
It means learning something new.
It means trying something new.

The unknown can be scary, but don't let it make you live life small. You were made to live a great life. So, live your definition of "big" (even if that means living a simple life).

So, what does your ideal life look like? Define it, visualize it daily, and most importantly, take action to bridge the gap between your current and desired selves. The growth needed to achieve your dreams is the space between where you are today and where you need to be.

What are the books you need to read? Who are the people you need to meet? What training do you need to receive? The lifestyle you need to live to close that gap between who you are now and who you need to be?

You can look at those steps with either fear or excitement.

Consider this: The time it takes to respond with either fear or excitement to this journey is the same. Choose excitement and inspiration; it'll propel you further, and you'll have more fun along the way.

Which path will you choose?

💡 Exercise: Confront Your Fears

Create a list of things that frighten you, regardless of their size. Once your list is complete, make it a habit to confront your fears daily. Begin with small steps. If you're afraid to try sushi, give it a shot. If you're hesitant to ask someone out, leap. If public speaking terrifies you, face it. Afraid to dance? Get out on the dance floor.

The more you challenge your fears, the more you'll discover they weren't as intimidating as you once believed.

"To conquer fear, there is but one path: action. Excellence hinges on the nurturing of daily habits, the firm establishment of routines, and an unyielding commitment to consistency.

For those who yearn for success beyond their wildest dreams, dare to venture beyond the confines of your comfort zone. It is within the learning and growth zone that the person you've always aspired to become awaits."

–Lan Phan

STEP BEYOND YOUR COMFORT ZONE

Have you ever felt that gnawing fear in your stomach when trying something new?

I have, too.

That fear signifies growth, learning, and expanding beyond your comfort zone.

The comfort zone feels secure because it's familiar, but it can also keep us stuck in the status quo. Imposter syndrome, fear, procrastination, and insecurity thrive in this fear zone. You cannot chase your dreams, grow, or fulfill your purpose while trapped there; it's simply not possible.

What you desire lies beyond fear. It's on the other side of your comfort zone where you'll find the learning and growth zones. To escape the fear zone, you must act, create daily habits, establish routines, and keep moving forward even when fear lingers.

Here's a little secret: Your body doesn't differentiate between fear and excitement. So, the next time you feel that stomach-churning feeling, tell yourself it's excitement. You're excited to apply for that job, to speak in public, or to ask someone out.

Sometimes, you need to act despite your fear. Do it while you're afraid. Do it while your hands tremble.

The next time will be a little less scary. Over time, it becomes a habit, and eventually, it becomes who you are.

SLAY THE DAY

"You're not going to master the rest of your life in one day. Just relax. Master the day. Then just keep doing that every day."
—Unknown

Take a step back and take a deep breath. Be kind to yourself.

Transformation doesn't happen overnight. Instead, focus on conquering the day. Start by hydrating with eight cups of water, completing at least one crucial task before noon, taking a refreshing walk in nature, and embracing moments of meditation.

Remember, you can achieve all that is meant for you, but it won't happen in a single day. Rome wasn't built in a day. The grandest achievements are constructed through a lifetime of small daily decisions encompassing habits, relationships, and mindset.

We tend to overestimate what we can achieve in a day and underestimate what we can accomplish in a lifetime. The key is to prioritize mastering each day, one by one, and then continue this journey of growth and progress.

💡 Exercise: Unlock Success with a Steadfast Morning Routine

To set a positive tone for your day, it's vital to establish and sustain a consistent morning routine. The key to maximizing the potential of your mornings lies in unwavering consistency.

Delve into Hal Elrod's "Miracle Morning" principles to craft a fulfilling morning ritual. You can pick up his book or watch his talk on YouTube.

This steadfast practice will empower you to approach each day with renewed positivity and clear intention.

CHANGE IS MESSY, DO IT ANYWAY

"Change is hard at first, messy in the middle, and gorgeous at the end."
—Robin Sharma

Embrace the profound truth that your life undergoes a remarkable transformation when you summon the courage to step beyond the confines of your comfort zone and embrace personal growth.

While it's often said that fortune favors the bold, true success rewards those who consistently put in the work and effort. This journey can look like personal development, healing past wounds, or an unwavering commitment to self-improvement. To attract success, you must evolve into someone who truly deserves it.

Consider this: A direct link connection exists between unwavering consistency and the seemingly magical occurrence we call luck. Those who steadfastly work on self-improvement tend to encounter a multitude of fortunate opportunities. Is this a mere coincidence? I think not.

So, if you yearn for change, remember that change begins from within you. Internalize this message and etch it to memory.

Is change challenging? Undoubtedly, but so is suffocating in places you've long outgrown.

Refuse to let your fears shackle your growth. Do not let your fears become your ceiling in life. You are more than capable of achieving greatness. You are already great.

💡 Exercise: Discover Your Path to Personal Growth for Fulfilling Your Dreams

Pinpoint the precise areas of personal development essential for attaining your aspirations. Proactively take steps to acquire the knowledge and skills you need.

The internet offers a treasure trove of inspirational resources and learning opportunities, often without the financial burden of tuition fees or substantial training costs.

EMBRACE IMPERFECTION

"Fear has two meanings, forget everything and run, or
face everything and rise. The choice is yours."
–Zig Ziglar

The life you've always wanted is on the other side of fear and procrastination. More often than not, the latter is a consequence of the former.

Often, this fear is tied to our need for perfection. As someone who has grappled with perfectionism, I can intimately relate. I missed out on countless opportunities due to my fear of failure. I used to think, "If I can't do it perfectly, I won't do it at all."

Sure, I appeared proficient when tackling activities, I had mastered, but what might my life look like if I had taken more risks? What would I be doing if I didn't let my fears and need for imperfection get in the way of trying something new? What adventures have I missed out on because I didn't let myself fail at something new?

💡 Exercise: Embrace Imperfection and Overcome Fear

Take a few moments to think about instances when you avoided trying something new or pursuing a goal because of a fear of imperfection or failure. Consider how these instances may have limited your experiences and opportunities.

Choose one activity or endeavor you've been longing to try but have been hesitant to because of fear or perfectionism. It could be a new hobby, a skill you want to acquire, a project you want to start, or an adventure you'd like to embark upon.

Set a Specific Goal: Define a clear and achievable goal for the chosen endeavor. Make sure the goal is specific, measurable, and time bound. For example, if you want to start painting, your goal could be: "Complete one small painting within the next two weeks."

Acknowledge Imperfection: Embrace the idea that it's okay to make mistakes and that imperfection is part of the learning process. Remember the saying, "Done is better than perfect."

Plan Your First Step: Break your goal into smaller, manageable steps. Create a detailed plan of action, including a timeline for each step.

Commit to taking the first step toward your goal. Schedule a specific time to engage in the activity or start the project. Hold yourself accountable to this commitment.

When you start working on your chosen endeavor, remember that the journey is just as important, if not more so, than the destination. Allow yourself to enjoy the process without fixating on achieving perfection.

After completing your first step, take a moment to reflect on the experience. What did you learn? How did it feel to embrace imperfection? Use this reflection to adjust your plan and continue progressing toward your goal.

As you become more comfortable embracing imperfection and overcoming fear, apply this mindset to other areas of your life. Challenge yourself to try new things and pursue opportunities without being hindered by the fear of failure.

Remember that growth often occurs outside your comfort zone, and stumbling is okay. Embracing imperfection can lead to personal development, increased confidence, and a more prosperous, more fulfilling life.

CHANGE REQUIRES CHANGING WHO WE ARE

The Art of Becoming: Change and Letting Go of What We Are No Longer

Growth is a Journey of Becoming

The path to self-discovery and personal transformation isn't a destination; it's a lifelong journey. Unlike the structured progression of school, where you work hard for a set number of years and receive a degree as your reward, the transformation of your life is an ongoing process. There is no finish line. It demands intentional and meaningful changes to enhance your well-being, accomplish your goals, and find fulfillment.

This journey is dynamic, evolving as you progress through different stages of life. The person you aspired to be in your twenties may differ significantly from who you strive to become in your forties. It's essential to recognize that becoming authentic is a lifelong pursuit that ideally leads to greater wisdom and authenticity as you age.

The Art of Becoming Requires Two Things

We often perceive change as a complex equation, yet it essentially boils down to two fundamental elements: 1) what we incorporate into our lives and 2) what we remove from our lives. To take it back to grade school math (prior to Core Math, that shit is hard), it's about addition (+) and subtraction (-).

We already covered much of what you can add or incorporate into your life during Secret 2: Your Mindset Creates Your Destiny and Secret 3: Change Requires Consistent Action. Initiating any change begins with cultivating the right mindset. Moreover, genuine progress emerges through consistent, purposeful action. The journey of becoming demands that we start before we are ready. It compels us to confront challenges head-on, to persevere unwaveringly, even when faced with adversity—which, inevitably we will. It requires that we invest effort daily even when things get hard, which it will. It requires that with each attempt, we do our best to get a tiny bit better than yesterday. That's the essence of becoming.

There's no "faking it till you make it." You must: *DO IT DAILY* until you become it.

Letting Go of What We Are No Longer

The path of growth and self-improvement not only characterizes transformation but is equally marked by the act of letting go of what no longer benefits us. I frequently find solace in the profound words of author Toni Morrison, who once proclaimed, "You wanna fly? You gotta give up the shit that weighs you down."

During my freshman year at Stanford University, I contemplated dropping out of school because I felt woefully unprepared. Understanding my hardship, my friend imparted this very quote to me. It served as a poignant reminder that I needed to shed the layers of insecurity and imposter syndrome that were holding me back and instead embrace my own strength and potential: I had to drop the shit that weighed me down.

Transformation is about becoming a better version of ourselves and letting go of that which hinders our growth and well-being. Among the things we must relinquish are harmful self-talk, insecurity, toxic relationships, lingering regrets, the fear of failure, the unattainable pursuit of perfection, unhealthy habits, and unrealistic expectations, among others.

Letting go is an indispensable process in the pursuit of positive transformation. It demands both time and effort, yet in shedding what no longer nurtures our growth and well-being, we create the fertile ground for constructive change and personal evolution.

Becoming Your Best Self

Becoming the best version of yourself is an endless endeavor. It's not defined by a single action but rather a culmination of consistent efforts that begin with Secret 1: Identifying What Matters Most. This involves deep self-reflection to understand your core values. Once you have clarity on your values, setting goals that align with them becomes your guiding principle—the North Star that directs your path.

From there, you delve into Secret 2: Your Mindset. Cultivating a growth mindset becomes paramount. This mindset seeks learning opportunities, embraces challenges, and views failures as steppingstones toward growth. With a crystal-clear vision of your desired life, you move on to Secret 3: Action. Transformation requires consistent action. During this phase, you implement changes aligned with your goals and vision. Establishing habits and systems that foster success becomes vital.

Finally, Secret 4: You arrive at the Art of Becoming: Change Requires Changing Who We Are, understanding there is no finish line. It's about continuous learning and resilience. It's about shedding what no longer serves us, as much as it's about becoming who we were always meant to be. It's about building a supportive community that nurtures your growth and distancing yourself from those that do not. It's about surrounding yourself with people who align with the person you are becoming.

Becoming Trumps Motivation

Change is exhilarating at first, but motivation tends to wane over time. Remember those New Year's resolutions that fizzled out quickly? We often fixate on the plateau and must remember the mountain we've climbed. This fourth section emphasizes the art of becoming. We must combine newfound knowledge to make genuine change and create daily habits and systems that sustain our transformation.

In essence, change is the process of becoming, and becoming is the result of doing. It's a journey that demands a mindset shift, action, and unwavering consistency. While growth and transformation are undoubtedly challenging, what's even more demanding is failing to evolve into the person you're meant to be due to fear or a reluctance to put in the effort.

Becoming and the Power of Your Community

One essential aspect of 'becoming' that deserves its own category is the power of your community. As I've often said, we are, indeed, the sum of the people we surround ourselves with. Therefore, it's crucial that we choose wisely. The role of community in our personal transformation journey cannot be overstated. It possesses the potential to either ignite personal growth and positive change or, conversely, to cast a detrimental influence on our path.

I know this lesson painfully well having experienced it firsthand during my freshman year of high school. At that time, I fell in with the wrong crowd, and tragically, the loss of a friend to a drive-by shooting altered the course of my life. Instead of continuing down a perilous path of affiliations with gang members and cutting class, I redirected my focus toward academics and athletics. I surrounded myself with friends who encouraged and challenged me to excel in these areas.

Whether you're pursuing personal development, a career change, a fitness goal, or any other transformative endeavor, the support and camaraderie of a community can be a true game changer. It serves as a reassuring reminder that you are not alone on your journey and that together, you can achieve remarkable transformations. Whether online or in person, finding or creating a community that aligns with your goals can be a powerful catalyst for personal growth and positive change. This is the reason why I created the Community of Seven. I couldn't find my community, so I created one.

Empowering Others to Discover Their Purpose

Service to others and empowerment is the key to unlocking one's purpose, and it extends beyond personal development—it involves uplifting those around you. However, this is not a one-time endeavor; it's a daily commitment.

Embark on your purpose-driven journey today, but don't stop there. Tomorrow, do it again and keep doing it consistently. The true power lies in sustained dedication.

Yet don't restrict your transformation solely to yourself. Extend your hand to others, guiding them to discover and live their purposes. By lifting others, we lift ourselves. Through unity, we create a ripple effect of positive change, collectively shaping the world we aspire to see.

So, as you embark on your purpose-driven path, remember that real impact arises not just from your personal growth but from inspiring and supporting those around you in finding and living their purpose.

Together, we can change the world.

"We cannot become what we want by clinging to old habits. Change takes change. Change takes changing who we are. Becoming the person you aspire to be requires unwavering, daily, and consistent action."

–Lan Phan

EXCELLENCE REQUIRES DAILY ACTION

To attain excellence, you must ignite an unrelenting fire for change within yourself. It can't merely be a desire; it must be a hunger that remains insatiable until you reach your goals.

However, wanting and wishing is not enough. Yearning for a better life won't magically bring it to fruition. To achieve your aspirations, you must marry that fervent desire with resolute and purposeful action. It is in doing that our future takes shape. Actual progress is born from bold, calculated, and purpose-driven actions.

Those familiar but unproductive habits you hold on to are like heavy chains holding you back from your true potential. It's time to break free from what's holding you back. Let go of that which is weighing you down. Shed the cloak of complacency, and step confidently into your future by committing to daily action.

In this arena, you become the architect of your destiny and the creator of your best self. Always remember excellence is not a passive pursuit; it demands action. Seize the day and create the future you desire!

YOU ARE NOT YOUR PAST

"Never be a prisoner of your past. It was just a lesson, not a life sentence."
—Robin Sharma

Don't let your past dictate who you are in the present. Instead, see your past as a precious lesson that propels your growth rather than a binding sentence that forces you to relive prior mistakes.

This concept is akin to a story I once heard from a friend. She had a client who she thought disliked her due to the way he spoke to her: curt and abrupt.

When she addressed this with him, he was perplexed.

He clarified that it wasn't her; he simply didn't think he was a "good speaker."

Curious, my friend asked why he held this belief.

He recounted a childhood memory of a second-grade teacher who had asked him to read aloud to the class. The teacher swiftly labeled him a bad speaker when he attempted to read.

My friend looked at him and posed a question, "Who's telling you that now?"

After a moment of contemplation, he exclaimed, "Me."

How many of us have been programmed at an early age that we're not good enough, too loud, not skinny enough, fill in the blank?

To truly grow and progress to the next phase of our lives, we must let go of the story we've been telling ourselves. Stories that others have written for us in the past. Those stories don't belong to us. Let them go.

Remember, the past and future are all mental states that exist solely in the realm of your thoughts. Actual existence lies in the present moment—embracing the past as a teacher, the present as your canvas, and the future as an unwritten chapter.

Never forget that the present moment is the one thing that truly exists in this world. You always have the power to rewrite your own story.

💡 Exercise: Letting Go of Your Past Stories

Take a moment to identify a narrative from your past that you must relinquish to become the person you aspire to be. Reflect on its origins and ask yourself, "Who planted this story in my mind? Was it my parents, a teacher, or perhaps a friend?"

Often, our beliefs are imprinted on us during our formative years. To progress to the next chapter of our lives, we must shed the narratives that have defined us.

Once you've identified the negative narrative, write it down on paper. Then, symbolically, let it go by burning it. Whenever you recite this negative story, remember that you've released it and are rewriting your narrative. That past story no longer has the power to define you.

Embrace your potential for growth and move forward."

BAGGAGE YOU DON'T NEED TO CARRY

RELEASE THE WEIGHT OF YOUR PAST

Why do you bear the weight of the world on your shoulders? It's time to set it free. Progressing toward your dreams becomes far more manageable when you unburden yourself from the emotional baggage you've carried.

I once was a "bag" lady when I was younger. The weight of guilt pressed heavily, and I shouldered the demands of others, unaware of the importance of reciprocity. I allowed takers to drain me until my well ran dry. Regrets from the past and fears of the future became constant companions, like the security blanket I clung to as a child.

With age and wisdom, I understood that I wasn't solely responsible for this load. So, I began to share the burden with my loved ones. I abandoned bags that were never mine to carry. I relinquished bags that no longer aligned with the person I was becoming. I broke generational curses and forged generational wealth. I evolved into the person they once said I couldn't become.

Growth takes many forms, and it's not just about becoming; it's also about shedding what no longer serves you. It means releasing the baggage you no longer need to carry.

KEEP DOING WHAT SCARES YOU

*"Too many of us are not living our dreams because
we are living our fears."*
—Les Brown

Are you pursuing your dreams or yielding to your fears?

Maya Angelou, the renowned poet, once wisely said, "Hope and fear cannot occupy the same space...invite one to stay."

Today, challenge yourself to do something that scares you, even if it's the last thing you want to do:

Display vulnerability at work.
Speak up in a meeting.
Ask for that long-awaited promotion.
Apply for that job.
Build a business.
Ask someone out on a date.
Belt out a song at the top of your lungs during karaoke.

Remember, courage isn't the absence of fear; it's the ability and willingness to confront your fears head-on, even when your heart races and your palms sweat. Embrace the paradox that as you repeatedly face your fears, they gradually lose their power, leaving you stronger and more confident.

💡 Exercise: Conquering Your Fears Exercise

- Start by listing three things that genuinely scare you, whether related to your personal or professional life. These should be challenges that, if overcome, would bring you closer to your dreams or aspirations.
- For each fear you've identified, outline a clear and actionable plan for confronting it. Break down the steps you need to take and

set achievable milestones for each. Remember, starting small and progressively working your way up is vital.

- Keep a journal to record your experiences as you confront these fears. Document how you felt before and after taking action and any lessons learned.
- As you begin to tackle your fears, celebrate each small victory. Recognize that even the act of facing your fears is a significant accomplishment.
- Continue to confront your fears and gradually work your way through your list. Periodically review your progress and reflect on how much you've grown and how your fears have diminished.

Remember that it's normal to feel apprehensive when confronting your fears, but the more you do it, the more empowered and resilient you become. Embrace the challenge, and watch how it leads you closer to your dreams.

"While we often want overnight success, the reality is that meaningful transformation takes time. In truth, success is born from the steady accumulation of small daily actions done consistently."

–Lan Phan

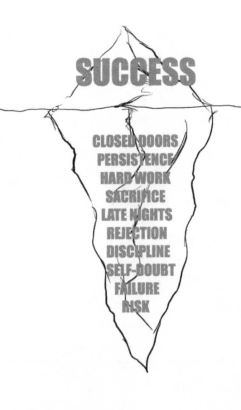

We crave instant change and overnight success but change seldom unfolds in a sudden burst of success.

Success, when it happens, may appear deceptively effortless to those observing from the sidelines. They aren't privy to the hundreds of tireless hours you dedicate to honing your craft. They didn't witness the stack of rejection letters that could fill a library. They couldn't comprehend the personal sacrifices you made to reach your current position.

The truth is that success unfolds through the accumulation of small, daily decisions consistently made. Many of these choices might seem inconsequential at the time, barely registering on the radar. Only when you look back, a month, a year, or even a decade later, can you truly grasp the immense growth that has transpired.

The secret lies in committing yourself to self-improvement every day until it becomes your identity. It entails making better daily choices, allowing them to cement themselves as habits. Over time, these habits transform into a systematic approach that sculpts you into the person you've always aspired to become.

This is the essence of change: gradual, persistent, and unyielding. Those tales of overnight success? They often unravel as little more than myths. Instead, redirect your focus toward daily self-improvement, and you'll find that real change is built brick by brick, with consistency as your cornerstone.

DARE TO GROW

"You cannot be committed to your dream and your comfort zone."
—Unknown

To truly pursue your dream, you must prioritize growth over comfort. Transformation doesn't occur within the boundaries of your comfort zone. Why? The status quo resides there and is taking up a lot of space.

Real change necessitates a shift in who you are. This transformation can be uncomfortable because it involves venturing into uncharted territory. It requires embracing the risk of failure, navigating unfamiliar terrain, leaving behind the past, and carving a new path. It means striving for improvement even when faced with difficulties. It's about evolving into the person you need to be to realize your most audacious dreams.

Undoubtedly, it won't be easy. But you know what's even more scary? Remaining in the same place you are today, five years from now, pondering the "what ifs." It's failing to reach your full potential because you were too scared to shine, too afraid to be exceptional, too hesitant to become the remarkable individual you were destined to be. Never forget; you weren't placed on this Earth to be mediocre. So, rise!

Chase your dreams till they become a typical day.

💡 Exercise: How can you shift from your comfort zone to the realm of learning and growth?

Perhaps by enrolling in a class, asking for that promotion, or pinpointing a specific action to propel yourself forward. Identify your chosen action and formulate a plan.

"To truly embrace what matters most in your life, you must become proficient in saying 'No' to commitments that do not align with your purpose."

–Lan Phan

SAY "NO"

If you're feeling burnt out, exhausted, or overwhelmed, it's crucial to embrace the power of the word "No."

As a recovering people pleaser, I understand this can pose a challenge. However, it's crucial to remember that time is a finite resource—there are only so many hours in a day, days in a year, and years in our lives.

When we master the art of saying "No," we are essentially saying "Yes" to what truly matters to us. That translates into prioritizing our family and friends and building our business.

I've ceased attempting to respond to every email, take on every project, or acquiesce to every request for a phone call. I've shed the guilt associated with saying "No" because I've come to recognize the limitations of my time. I think about my daughter and how saying "No" sometimes translates to saying "Yes" to quality time with her.

Let me emphasize this: Saying "No" is a way to say "Yes" to what holds importance in your life.

It's also vital to acknowledge those who may feel trapped, unable to utter "No" due to financial constraints or a lack of autonomy. I've found myself in that situation before. If you currently find yourself there, consider saying "Yes" to what is essential until you can eventually say "No." Subsequently, seek out areas in your life that can be shed—toxic relationships, detrimental habits, or oppressive work environments.

Learning to say "No" to things that no longer serve you creates space for positivity to flow in.

Identify three areas in which you can confidently say "No" at this moment, liberating time for what genuinely matters to you. Once identified, contemplate the possibility of excising them from your life.

CREATE SYSTEMS

"You will not always be motivated, so you must learn to be disciplined."
—Unknown

Positive affirmations don't work.
Motivation works but doesn't last.

You must marry your aspirations with concrete actions to reach your goals and foster lasting change.

The journey to personal growth requires discipline coupled with daily, systematic habits. What you do daily shapes your character and creates the person you evolve into. When you align your purpose, your "why," with unwavering consistency, you empower yourself to undergo a profound transformation.

Regardless of who you are trying to become or the goals you're trying to achieve, remember this: You can transform your life at any moment. It hinges on your willingness to do whatever you need to become the person you aspire to be. That evolution is made possible through your daily actions done consistently. Keep forging ahead, and let your unwavering determination illuminate your path forward.

💡 Exercise: How can you establish effective systems and habits that bring you closer to fulfilling your purpose?

Begin with modest steps but maintain unwavering consistency. Incrementally nurture these habits until they seamlessly integrate into your daily routine. Resist the urge to adopt a new habit until the one you're cultivating feels as instinctive as brushing your teeth.

"Be around
people who feel like
sunshine–people who bring
positivity, warmth, and
light into your life.
Surround yourself
with individuals
who contribute
to your mental and
emotional well-being."

–Lan Phan

BE AROUND PEOPLE WHO FEEL LIKE SUNSHINE

Life is too short and precious to be spent in the company of those who bring harm, stress, or pain into your world. Instead, surround yourself with people who feel like sunshine—people who bring positivity, warmth, and light into your life. Surround yourself with individuals who contribute to your mental and emotional well-being.

While it may not always be within our control to eliminate the takers and toxic influences from our lives, we hold the power to make conscious and deliberate choices about the relationships we prioritize. Doing so will pave the way for personal growth, happiness, and a more fulfilling life.

The deliberate act of curating our relationships holds significance across all facets of our lives. It encompasses choosing a life partner who shares our values and supports our personal growth, nurturing friendships built on trust, respect, and mutual support, and recognizing the importance of a positive work environment when making career decisions.

Remember, if a relationship costs you your inner peace, it is not worth it. You don't need that negativity in your life. Stay clear from people who drain you; don't let them bring their darkness into your life. They can take their negativity elsewhere, while you bask in the glow of your friends who feel like sunshine.

💡 Exercise: Cultivating Healthy Relationships

This exercise encourages you to intentionally nurture positive relationships and minimize the impact of stressful ones.

- List three individuals who consistently contribute to your mental and emotional well-being. Reflect on why their presence is uplifting and supportive in your life.
- Commit to spending more quality time with these positive individuals. Consider activities or conversations that strengthen your connection and well-being.

- List three people who tend to bring stress or negativity into your world. Reflect on specific situations or interactions that trigger anxiety.
- While avoiding these individuals altogether may not always be possible, commit to setting healthy boundaries when interacting with them. Decide on strategies to protect your mental and emotional space during these interactions.
- Consider creating mental and physical distance from individuals who consistently bring stress if circumstances allow. This may involve limiting your exposure or minimizing their impact on your life.
- Regardless of the nature of your relationships, prioritize self-care and well-being. Nurture yourself mentally and emotionally to build resilience against stressors.
- Periodically review and adjust your commitments and boundaries as needed. Ensure that you prioritize your mental and emotional health in your relationships.

This exercise empowers you to be mindful of the people you surround yourself with and take proactive steps to safeguard your mental and emotional well-being. It acknowledges that while complete avoidance may not always be possible, setting boundaries and prioritizing positive influences can significantly improve your overall quality of life.

Everyone's Growth
Looks Different

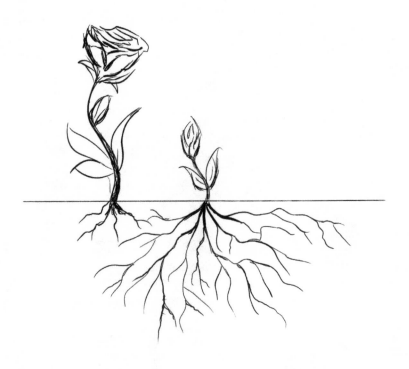

"You can't always judge growth on the surface level. Just because you can't see it doesn't mean it's not happening. Everyone's growth looks different."

–Lan Phan

DON'T FAKE IT TILL YOU MAKE IT, BECOME IT

In my twenties, I once subscribed to the notion of "fake it till I make it," believing that projecting confidence alone would lead me to my goals. However, it took only a short time to realize that mere pretense was insufficient; true success required genuine transformation. And the latter required action.

To embark on this journey, I committed to a deliberate process:

- Hard Work: I understood the need to put in the hard work, day in and day out.
- Continuous Learning: I became a perpetual learner, absorbing knowledge and insights.
- Embracing Growth: Personal growth became a core aspect of my life, a daily endeavor.
- Daily Growth: Striving to be better each day.
- Embracing Failure: I made peace with failure, recognizing it as a valuable teacher.

Persistence became my ally, and progress became my goal. I understood the importance of shedding anything that hindered my transformation, whether it was people, roles, or environments that didn't contribute to my growth.

So, remember, don't fake it till you make it. Instead, become the person you aspire to be through daily dedication and an unwavering commitment to your growth.

💡 Exercise: Crafting Your Future Self

Have you considered who you genuinely aspire to become? What steps must you take to metamorphose into that individual?

For instance, if your goal is to become a great friend, certain qualities are imperative: genuine interest in others, effective communication, high reliability, and unwavering loyalty. To reach this ideal, strive to embody the qualities you value in a friend.

But after addressing these initial questions, the most pivotal phase awaits and that is acting. Your aspirations and knowledge alone won't suffice. You must translate your desires into tangible actions. You must evolve into the person you aspire to be. Whether your ambition is to lead the free world or be an exemplary parent, identify the prerequisites for that role and take the necessary steps and actions to actualize your transformation.

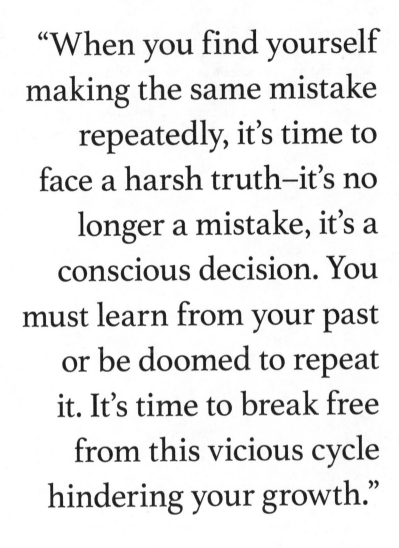

"When you find yourself making the same mistake repeatedly, it's time to face a harsh truth–it's no longer a mistake, it's a conscious decision. You must learn from your past or be doomed to repeat it. It's time to break free from this vicious cycle hindering your growth."

–Lan Phan

LEARN FROM YOUR MISTAKES

When you find yourself making the same mistake repeatedly, it's time to face a harsh truth—it's no longer a mere mistake; it has morphed into a conscious choice.

Understand this—making mistakes is a natural part of life. No one can fault you for making mistakes. It's literally a prerequisite for growth and self-development. However, if you find yourself making the same mistake on repeat, friend, that's on you.

We must take responsibility for our actions when we refuse to learn from our mistakes. We can't repeat past actions that got us into our current predicament and expect things to magically be different the next time around.

Are you going back to that toxic friendship? Are you getting back with your emotionally abusive ex? Are you not enforcing boundaries with the takers in your life? I'm sorry to say it, but that's all on you.

Indeed, change is painful and challenging. But what's worse is not learning from our experience and perpetually replaying the same scenario while hoping for things to be different this time around.

Genuine growth emerges when we can learn from our mistakes. This process can be painful and arduous, but the seeds for our transformation lie within it. To evolve, you must be open to adaptation, prepared to shift your course, and chart new directions. In short, stop doing the same shit and expecting a different result. Embrace a different strategy.

KEEP QUESTIONING YOUR HABITS

"Ask yourself if what you're doing today
is getting you closer to where you want to be tomorrow."
—Paulo Coelho

What books are you reading?
Who are you spending the most time with?
What are you consuming? Physically and mentally?
Are you creating boundaries and setting expectations for those around you?
Have you taken care of yourself through good sleep, exercise, and nutrition?

Remember this fundamental truth: our actions today mold who we become tomorrow. Each choice, no matter how seemingly insignificant, serves as a silent vote cast in favor of the person we will eventually become.

💡 Purpose Alignment Exercise: Charting Your Path to Your Dreams

Ask yourself if your habits, lifestyle, and decisions are getting you closer to living your purpose and achieving your dreams. If the answer is no, create new practices and systems.

In your journal or on a blank piece of paper, write down your answers to the following questions:

- What habits do I feel do not align with my purpose and dreams?
- How does my lifestyle support or hinder my progress toward my dreams?
- Are there any decisions I've made recently that may be taking me away from my desired path?

Close your eyes and visualize your ideal life where you live your purpose and achieve your dreams. Imagine every detail—your environment, relationships, daily routines, and overall sense of fulfillment.

Based on your reflection and visualization, identify at least three new practices or systems you can implement to align your life more closely with your purpose and dreams. Be specific and actionable.

Write a commitment statement in your journal, declaring your intention to make these changes. Create a simple action plan that outlines how you will integrate these new practices or systems into your daily life. Set achievable milestones and deadlines.

Set aside time each week to review your progress and make any necessary adjustments to your practices and systems. Keep a journal to track your journey and celebrate your successes. Remember that personal growth and alignment with your purpose are ongoing processes.

"If we are the sum of the people we spend the most time with, let us spend it with people who uplift us, inspire us, and move us forward."

–Lan Phan

MESSAGE FOR GIVERS

"If you're a giver, remember to learn your limits
because the takers don't have any."
–Henry Ford

The world is full of givers and takers. Giving is undoubtedly a beautiful act. It becomes less so when it leaves you feeling depleted. It's essential not to let the takers in the world drain your energy and leave you bitter.

Our surroundings and the people we choose to spend our time with, either by choice or circumstance, profoundly impact the people we become. Therefore, it is vital that we consciously surround ourselves with people who actively contribute to our growth.

If this is true, it becomes evident that we should prioritize relationships that uplift, inspire, and encourage us to move forward.

Should you find yourself consistently drained and depleted after interactions with a particular individual, it may be an opportune moment to reassess the nature of that friendship or association.

Remember that we have the power to set boundaries. Doing so protects our well-being and mental health and teaches people how to treat us. Choose relationships that nurture and support the person you aspire to become. In doing so, you create fertile ground for personal growth and fulfillment.

💡 Exercise: Assess Your Social Circles

Take some time to reflect on the people you spend the most time within your life. This could include friends, family members, coworkers, or acquaintances. Consider how each individual makes you feel after spending time with them.

- Create a list of the people who consistently uplift and inspire you, leaving you with positive energy. Note down those who drain your energy and leave you feeling depleted or bitter.
- For each person on your list, reflect on specific interactions or situations where you've experienced these emotions.
- Identify one or more individuals who may be takers in your life, draining your energy. Think about setting clear boundaries or limiting your exposure to them when necessary.
- Reach out to those who uplift and inspire you, expressing your appreciation for their positive influence. Strengthen these connections and consider spending more time with them.

By taking this inventory of your social circles, you can better understand the dynamics and decide which relationships to prioritize for your overall well-being and personal growth.

"Happiness has always
been a choice,
not a checklist."

–Lan Phan

BE HAPPY NOW

Stop waiting for the right time to be happy. That moment is now.

Quit waiting to celebrate until you land your dream job, acquire your degree, meet the perfect partner, or reach the pinnacle of financial stability. Choose joy now. Happiness has always been a choice, not a checklist.

Happiness resides in the present moment, embracing and cherishing the abundance already in your life. It doesn't dwell on past troubles or fret about an uncertain future.

Embrace the current moment. Savor the small moments of joy, whether as simple as a child's laughter, the warm smile of a loved one, or the changing colors of autumn leaves.

Recognize that happiness is a treasure you possess at this very moment. Our time on this earth is limited; do not postpone or delay, waiting for life to get easier because it won't. Life will always be complicated and nuanced. The perfect time to live and chase your dreams has always been now.

Happiness is meant to be lived in the present moment, not deferred until we get what we want.

Find joy. Now.

CLAP FOR OTHERS

"Always clap for your friends, even if their dreams transpire before you."
—Eleni Sophia

Stop seeing others as competition. See them as inspiration. That person staring back at you in the mirror has always been your only competition.

Undoubtedly, life presents various arenas where competition is inevitable—academics, sports, work challenges, and more. Engage in these contests if they align with your ambitions, for you can't triumph in a race you don't join. However, it's essential to recognize that your mindset shapes your journey. Strive relentlessly to become the finest version of yourself, and success will naturally follow. Redirect your gaze from those who trail or precede you.

Oprah Winfrey once revealed that her breakthrough came when she ceased emulating Barbara Walters and concentrated on being the best Oprah Winfrey she could be.

Laser-focus your energy on personal growth and your unique path. Develop the systems and habits that will propel you forward. In the meantime, know I'll be your loudest cheerleader, Raindrops.

💡 Exercise: Cultivate the practice of celebrating the triumphs of others.

Set aside a moment this week to honor someone else's accomplishment. For example, my daughter likes to go to races to cheer on the runners, even when we don't know anyone running. Fun fact: Celebrating others triggers the release of dopamine in our brains. We physically benefit by celebrating others!

LEAD WITH KINDNESS

If you think you're leading and no one is following
you, then you're only taking a walk.
—John C. Maxwell

Managers who rely on fear for power cannot truly be considered leaders. Why? You cannot lead if no one wants to follow you.

So how do you inspire people to follow you willingly? It's surprisingly simple: Be kind yet competent.

Kindness is not a sign of weakness; rather, it represents an immense strength.

In some workplaces, behaviors like bravado, dominance, and cruelty are mistakenly seen as displays of "strength." However, these are often fragile forms of leadership, if they can even be called leadership. They usually stem from insecurity, thrive in environments of entitlement, and are steeped in self-loathing.

In contrast, kindness emerges from strong values, is bolstered by self-assurance, and radiates self-love.

Leaders who lead with kindness always have followers willing to stand beside them, no matter the challenges.

Such leaders possess empathy for their teams, offering guidance and support. They are quick to take responsibility when things go wrong and are the first to offer praise when things go right. They understand that their duty as a leader is to create more leaders.

It's important to note that leadership isn't defined by titles but by the presence of kindness and empathy, driven by courage and guided by vision.

Take pride in your capacity for kindness. Much like water in a stream that, over time, can erode and shape rock beds, your kindness has transformative power in a hardened world.

♥Exercise: Cultivating Kindness in Leadership

Take some time to reflect on your past experiences with leaders or managers. Consider those who displayed kindness and empathy and note how it influenced your perception of them and your willingness to follow their lead.

Now, reflect on your values. What values do you hold dear? How do they align with the concept of kindness in leadership? Write down these values.

Assess your leadership style honestly. Do you tend to lean toward a more authoritarian, fear-driven approach, or do you embrace kindness and empathy in your leadership? Be critical but compassionate with yourself.

Now, choose a specific project, team, or situation where you can implement empathy in your leadership. Identify three actions or behaviors that align with kindness and empathy that you can apply in this context. For example, it could be actively listening to your team's concerns, providing constructive feedback, or acknowledging their achievements.

Approach at least two team members or colleagues you trust and ask for honest feedback on your leadership style. Encourage them to provide insights on whether they perceive kindness and empathy in your leadership and how it affects their work.

Take time to reflect on the outcomes and the responses from your team. Were there any noticeable improvements in collaboration, morale, or performance? What challenges did you face? Based on this, adapt your leadership approach as needed.

Commit to continuous improvement by regularly revisiting your leadership style and reinforcing kindness and empathy as core components. Set new goals and challenges to enhance your leadership skills further.

Don't overcomplicate networking and building strong professional relationships. Simply, just be a good person that cares about others and you will build relationships that last a lifetime."

–Lan Phan

BE A GOOD PERSON

At the core of building relationships lies a beautifully simple principle: caring. It's the art of pausing after asking how someone's doing and truly listening. This care extends beyond office walls, reaching into who a person is beyond their professional facade. It's about shared ground but also celebrating the differences.

We often overcomplicate professional relationships, yet it's as straightforward as being kind and genuinely concerned about someone's well-being and identity beyond work.

Amid life's complexities, the simplicity of genuine care fosters enduring and profound relationships. Simply, just be a good person and you will build relationships that last a lifetime.

BREAK THE CYCLE

"Be who you needed when you were younger."
—Brad Montague

Break the cycle.

Be the parent you needed when you were younger.

Be the boss you needed when you were younger.

Be the mentor you needed when you were younger.

Be the friend you needed when you were younger.

Be the teacher you needed when you were younger.

We can't change the past, but we can change ourselves and our actions.

Be the person you needed when you were younger.

When you break the cycle, you change yourself and those around you.

Let's break some generational curses today.

This is how we change the world, Raindrops.

💡 Exercise: Becoming Who You Needed Exercise: Breaking the Cycle

This exercise is designed to help you reflect on the support and guidance you needed when you were younger and encourage you to take action to become the person you need for others.

Reflecting on Your Past: Open your journal and write down the question: "Who did I need when I was younger?"

Reflect on the support, guidance, or role models you yearned for during your formative years. Explore various aspects of your life, including family, friendships, mentors, teachers, and other significant relationships. Be as specific as possible in your reflections.

Assessing Your Present. Ask yourself: "Am I embodying or providing this type of support to others?" Be honest and self-reflective.

Taking Action: From the support you wished for but aren't currently providing, choose one or more areas that resonate with you and that you're ready to work on. For each selected area, write down at least one concrete action you can take to start offering others the support you once longed for. These actions can range from small gestures, such as lending an empathetic ear, to more significant commitments, like mentoring or being a positive role model.

Making a Personal Commitment: Conclude your exercise by crafting a commitment statement. Declare your intention to take the actions you've identified in

Put your commitment into practice and record your experiences and progress in your journal. Regularly revisit your list of actions to gauge your growth in supporting others.

Remember that personal transformation is an ongoing journey. This exercise represents a meaningful step toward breaking the cycle and becoming the supportive presence others may need. Your actions can create a positive ripple effect, inspiring those around you to do the same.

DON'T MAKE THEIR ISSUES YOUR ISSUES

*"When you finally learn that a person's behavior has more to do with
their internal struggle than it ever did with you, you learn grace."*
—Alison Aars

It's Not About You. It's About Them (Mostly)

Occasionally, it might be about you, but that's not our primary focus here.

When confronted with rudeness, hatred, or hostility, it's a natural inclination to start self-blaming, questioning whether you must have done something wrong or, worse, believing you somehow deserved such treatment. However, let's dispel that notion right away.

Don't allow their negativity and pessimism to dampen your spirit. Remind yourself that this is their issue, not yours.

Hurt people tend to be proficient at hurting others, whether a stranger on a bus, a colleague at work, or even someone they might care deeply for.

Once you grasp that their negative behavior has nothing to do with you and is, in fact, a reflection of who they are and their inner struggles, their lousy behavior loses its power to ruin your day.

💡 **Exercise:** Think back to the last time you encountered negative behavior. Remind yourself that their behavior has nothing to do with you and everything to do with their internal struggles. Don't you dare give them the power to ruin your day by empowering their lousy behavior,

BUILD THE WORLD YOU WANT

"To all the doors that closed on me: I'm coming back to buy the building."
—Pinky Dior

I've stopped waiting to be picked, to be chosen, to be told that I am ready.

I know I'm ready.

I'm done with waiting for mere breadcrumbs when I know I deserve a seven-course meal.

I've stopped holding out for promotions that never materialize.

Instead, I'm taking matters into my own hands.

I'm making my own damn table.

I'm busy laying the foundation for generational wealth. I'm banishing family curses, determined to break free from the shackles of past family struggles.

I'm seizing control of my destiny, charting my unique course in life, and forging a path toward my dreams.

Together, let's dismantle systemic "isms" and build systemic equality. Let us construct a framework of true equality. Instead of fostering hatred, let us cultivate love and understanding among one another.

While some may choose to dwell in complacency, we can collectively shape the world we've longed for. Rather than striving to change what exists, let us unite to create the world we want to live in.

MAKE ROOM FOR GOOD PEOPLE

"Don't let anyone rent space in your head, unless they're a good tenant."
–Dr. Bill Crawford

Your mental well-being is too precious to let toxic individuals occupy your life and mental space. Elevate the standards and evict them. They don't deserve real estate in your mind.

If we are the sum of who we surround ourselves with, let us choose wisely— your perspective on life changes when your circle of influence changes.

Exercise discernment in selecting your friends and associates because they play a significant role in shaping the person you ultimately become.

💡 Exercise: Prioritizing Your Mental Well-being

- Start by embarking on a crucial exercise to enhance your mental health. Identify the individuals in your life who have a draining and exhausting effect on you after interactions with them.
- Delve deeper by asking yourself whether this draining behavior is occasional, possibly stemming from a temporary challenging phase in your life. For instance, a friend going through a tough time may need your mental support during that period.
- However, scrutinize whether this draining behavior is habitual, such as a friend who consistently criticizes your choices or frequently engages in gossip. In such cases, it may be essential to evaluate the impact of these individuals on your well-being and consider creating some distance.
- Reflect on the importance of preserving your own mental and emotional energy. While providing support during tough times is admirable, maintaining boundaries is equally crucial when dealing with individuals who continually drain your positivity and mental resilience.
- Consider the steps you can take to protect your mental well-being in these situations, which may include setting boundaries,

communicating your needs, or, in some cases, making the difficult decision to minimize your interactions with such individuals.

- Document your observations and decisions in a journal, tracking your progress in fostering a healthier and uplifting social environment.

This exercise is a valuable tool for safeguarding your mental health by identifying and addressing the individuals who may harm your well-being, allowing you to make informed choices about your social connections.

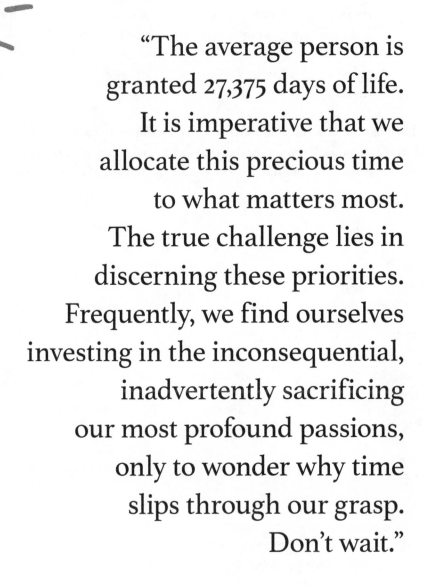

"The average person is
granted 27,375 days of life.
It is imperative that we
allocate this precious time
to what matters most.
The true challenge lies in
discerning these priorities.
Frequently, we find ourselves
investing in the inconsequential,
inadvertently sacrificing
our most profound passions,
only to wonder why time
slips through our grasp.
Don't wait."

–Lan Phan

PRIORITIZE YOUR HEALTH

What's at the top of your priority list? Is it your health and mental well-being?

If not, consider this: How can you effectively support others if you neglect your own well-being? Just like you can't pour from an empty cup, you can't assist others when you're sick, burned out, or exhausted.

When our cup runneth over, we are better equipped to help others. When we are abundant, healthy, and strong, we are in the best position to nurture and attend to the people and pursuits we hold dear.

It's important to understand that self-care is not selfish; it's as essential as fuel is to a car.

By prioritizing your physical and mental health, you equip yourself to offer better assistance to others. Much like how you meticulously schedule work meetings, don't forget to schedule time for exercise, self-care, and enjoyable activities. Set aside moments for shared meals with friends and family, disconnect from screens, and foster deeper, more meaningful connections. This is how we prioritize our well-being to help others.

YOUR LIFE IS ALREADY ABUNDANT

*"You already have everything you need to be content. Your
real work is to do whatever it takes to realize that."*
—Geneen Roth

I don't drive a fancy car. My house is smallish. My Instagram feed isn't meticulously curated to portray a perfect life.

However, I have a beautiful family that fills my heart with joy. I have friends that feel like family. I have a home that is filled with love. We have food on our table. I do meaningful work that uplifts others.

This is my definition of abundance. What does abundance mean to you?

Sometimes, we may feel lacking when we think about everything we want to accomplish on our life journey. Yet as we turn our gaze inward, we realize that our cup is already overflowing.

We just needed to pause and count our blessings.

💡 Exercise: Cultivating Gratitude in Your Life

Purpose: This exercise aims to deepen your gratitude and appreciation for the aspects of your life that bring you happiness and fulfillment.

Begin by listing three aspects of your life you are genuinely grateful for. These could encompass relationships, achievements, possessions, personal qualities, or any elements that bring joy and contentment.

Take a moment to focus on each item individually. If it helps, close your eyes to visualize more clearly. Consider why you appreciate and value each entry on your list. Reflect on its positive impact on your life and how it contributes to your well-being and happiness.

Now, expand your gratitude list to include at least five more things you are grateful for. Delve deeper and contemplate smaller, often overlooked aspects that add value to your life. As you add to your list, take your time to acknowledge and feel gratitude for each item honestly. Visualize how your life would differ without it.

Sit with Your Gratitude: Once you have completed your expanded list, take a moment to sit with the feelings of gratitude and contentment that arise within you. Allow yourself to fully embrace these emotions, acknowledging your gratitude for having these positive elements in your life.

This exercise encourages a profound appreciation for the various facets of your life that bring you happiness and fulfillment. It helps you recognize and celebrate the abundance of positive elements in your life, fostering a greater sense of contentment and gratitude.

SOMETIMES YOU NEED TO BORROW COURAGE

*"At times, our light goes out and is rekindled by a spark
from another person. Each of us has cause to think with deep
gratitude of those who have lighted the flame within us."*
—Albert Schweitzer

There will come moments when we must borrow courage. In times when the weight of our burdens becomes too much to bear, we must lean on our family, friends, and community to lift us up and rekindle the spark necessary to propel us forward.

Let us embrace the roles of both recipient and giver of this flame. Life's journey was never meant to be navigated alone; we are here to guide one another during our darkest hours.

The light is how we find one other. It holds equal significance to seeking help when needed and offering assistance when possible.

Don't hesitate to ask for support, seek out your community, and aspire to extend a helping hand while graciously receiving it.

Above all, let's nurture gratitude and profound appreciation for those who have illuminated our path and continue to do so.

💡 Exercise: Reflect on Your Support System

Reflect on the people who have been your pillars of strength and support during challenging times. Write down their names and consider the qualities that make them dependable sources of courage and encouragement.

Next, think about how you can reciprocate this support. What can you offer to be a source of inspiration and strength for others in your circle? Write down actionable steps to be there for your friends, family, or community when they need it most.

Finally, express your gratitude. Reach out to at least one person from your support system and tell them how much you appreciate their presence in your life. It could be a heartfelt message, a phone call, or a small gesture of kindness. Share your gratitude and strengthen your bonds.

ENCOURAGE OTHERS TO GROW

"The best teams are made up of nobodies who love everybody and serve anybody and don't care about becoming somebody."
–Phil Dooley

What I learned in team sports helped me succeed in corporate America. Let me tell you how.

In a world where everyone wants to be an influencer and a star, I've always enjoyed working in teams where people's egos are left at the threshold.

This doesn't imply relinquishing one's ambition and achievements. Quite the contrary, it entails bringing your genuine self to the table while acknowledging the significance of every voice in the room.

It means nurturing those voices, especially when they don't resound as loudly as yours.

It requires an understanding that each individual brings a unique contribution, and your role as a leader is to cultivate a culture founded on trust, motivation, and camaraderie.

When these three elements synergize seamlessly, the realm of possibilities becomes boundless.

💡 Exercise: Fostering an Inclusive Leadership Environment

As a leader, it's essential to introspect whether you're cultivating an atmosphere where everyone believes their voice is important. Do they genuinely feel that their thoughts and opinions carry weight?

During meetings, note whether the same voices consistently dominate the conversation. If this is the case, consider strategies to empower those more reserved to share their viewpoints. How can you create an environment of psychological safety where everyone feels comfortable contributing their best ideas?

Remember that leadership isn't synonymous with having all the answers; it's about empowering and inspiring others to discover solutions while evolving into their best selves.

CELEBRATE YOUR PROGRESS

"I'm Not Where I Want To Be, But I'm Where I Need To Be."
—Katie Licavoli

Take a moment to celebrate your progress. While you might not be where you want to be, remember that each step forward, no matter how small, brings you closer to your dreams.

Regardless of its scale, progress is worth celebrating at every juncture. There's no need to wait for unattainable perfection; instead, cultivate gratitude for each milestone as they have played an integral role in shaping the person you are today.

So, keep forging ahead. Keep thriving. While you may not have arrived at your destination, you have undoubtedly journeyed far beyond your previous point. Let's honor your progression.

I'm here, cheering you on every step of the way.

💡 Exercise: Reflecting on a Decade of Growth

Take a moment to journey back a full 10 years ago. Recall where you stood, your circumstances, and your person back then. Now, shift your focus to the present. Acknowledge the remarkable journey you've undertaken, the challenges you've conquered, and the strides you've made, both major and minor. With these reflections in mind, take a moment to visualize the path ahead, brimming with success and achievement. Picture your future self, embracing the culmination of your aspirations, knowing that every step you take brings you closer to your dreams.

CHOOSE THE RIGHT PEOPLE

*"When you start seeing your worth, you'll find it
harder to stay around people who don't."*
—Unknown

Never let anyone dim your light or take you for granted. This principle extends to all areas of life, including love, home, friendship, and work.

We teach people how to treat us. Read that again.

Teach people to treat you with the respect you deserve.

It starts with creating clear boundaries. It's maintained by standards and expectations. And when necessary, it ends by leaving situations that no longer serve you.

Don't let small people define your worth. Your time is far too precious for that.

And according to Jim Rohn, if we are the average of the 5 people we spend the most time with, let us choose to surround ourselves with healers, givers, protectors, and providers.

💡 **Exercise: Take a moment to consider the five individuals with whom you spend the most time.**

Do these connections serve as wellsprings of inspiration and motivation, propelling you forward on your path? If not, it could be worthwhile to assess the amount of time and energy you allocate to these relationships. If you find yourself depleted and fatigued after each interaction, it may be necessary to establish some distance from such individuals. As a more enduring objective, consider connecting with those who consistently uplift and bolster you in your quest for personal growth and happiness. If you find yourself invigorated and enthused after spending time with a particular person, it's likely a valuable relationship worth nurturing and dedicating your resources to. Life is too short to be spending it with people who make you feel terrible after every interaction.

YOU DESERVE RESPECT

"When you finally learn a person's behavior has more to do with their own internal struggle than it ever did with you...you learn Grace."
—Allison Aars

I'd like to share a perspective that has profoundly impacted my life. In my younger years, I often dwelled on perceived wrongdoings that led to my boss's disapproval or questioning my abilities when a coworker belittled my contributions. In my personal life, I clung to toxic relationships long past their expiration date, driven by a misguided sense of loyalty.

However, I've learned from these experiences that fixing anyone is not my responsibility. I am not obligated to carry the weight of their judgments or the consequences of their behavior toward me.

Of course, there have been times when I was genuinely at fault, and in those cases, I took ownership of my mistakes, learned from them, and strove to do better. After all, nobody is without fault, and personal growth often emerges from acknowledging our errors.

Yet there is another crucial aspect to consider. There are instances when people harbor negativity toward you for reasons unrelated to your actions. They may despise you simply for being yourself, for what you represent, or for characteristics you cannot change—such as your religion, skin color, gender, disability, or job title.

The critical insight here is that their hatred reflects their inner turmoil. It arises from the toxic lessons they have absorbed, which unfairly devalue those different from them.

Recognize that they may dislike you because they struggle to accept themselves. Their hatred is rooted in the damaging notion that different people are somehow less.

Understanding that you are not responsible for changing or contorting yourself to please them is crucial. Love yourself enough to step away from such negativity until respect is reciprocated. Extend grace by forgiving their behavior, recognizing that they may not know better, but also know that you deserve better.

💡 Exercise: Shifting Perspectives

Reflect on instances in your life when you may have misinterpreted someone's actions or when someone may have misunderstood your own.

Now, try to see the situation from the other person's perspective. What might have been going on in their life that influenced their actions or words? How might their internal struggles have played a role?

Reflect on the impact of misinterpretations on your relationships. Did it lead to misunderstandings, conflicts, or missed opportunities for connection? Write down any lessons you've learned from these experiences.

In your own life, consider times when others may have misinterpreted your actions or intentions. How did it make you feel? Were there underlying factors or personal struggles they might not have been aware of?

Think about how enhanced awareness of our internal struggles and those of others can foster compassion and better communication. How can you approach future situations with more empathy and understanding?

If you're comfortable, engage in a conversation with a trusted friend or family member about a specific instance where misunderstandings occurred. Share your perspective and ask for their insights on what might have been happening on their end.

Challenge yourself to practice empathy in your daily interactions. Before jumping to conclusions, consider what might be happening beneath the surface for the other person.

Remember, my friend, the more we learn to see through different lenses and understand the complexities within ourselves and others, the richer our connections become.

EMPOWER OTHERS

"To inspire people, don't show them your superpowers. Show them theirs."
—Alexander den Heijer

A title alone doesn't define leadership. Your actions and how you wield your power determine your leadership or the absence thereof.

As leaders within our homes, workplaces, and communities, our primary responsibility is cultivating and nurturing future leaders.

Our role involves:

Inspiring: We must serve as a wellspring of inspiration, igniting the passion and drive in those we lead.

Empowering: We must empower others to realize their fullest potential and excel in their pursuits.

Enriching the World: We are tasked with leaving a lasting, positive impact on the world, striving to improve it with our actions.

Legacy Building: Even when our journey ends, we aim to establish a legacy of influence that endures, shaping future generations.

Authentic leadership, fundamentally, is not self-centered. Instead, it centers on the collective growth of those we lead. Leadership's essence lies in elevating everyone in our sphere, motivating them to conquer the seemingly impossible.

Ask yourself: Are you actively empowering others and fostering the growth of new leaders?

Are you dedicated to building a culture grounded in trust and collaboration, where each team member can perform at their best?

To understand a company's culture, observe how those in leadership positions treat those with less power in the organization. This dynamic speaks volumes about the organization's culture or the absence thereof.

Remember that leadership isn't handed to you; it's something you earn through your actions and commitment to empowering others.

💡 Exercise: Leadership Reflection and Action Plan

Objective: To reflect on your leadership approach and identify areas for improvement in empowering others and fostering a culture of trust and collaboration.

Self-Assessment:

Begin by taking a moment to self-assess your leadership style. Consider recent interactions with your team, colleagues, or subordinates. Reflect on your actions and behaviors as a leader. Ask yourself:

- How do I empower and support team members to excel?
- Do I actively contribute to a culture of trust and collaboration?
- Am I dedicated to nurturing new leaders within the organization?
- Are there areas where my leadership may need to catch up?

Identify Strengths and Weaknesses:

Write down your strengths and areas where you excel as a leader in empowering others and fostering a positive culture. Additionally, acknowledge areas where you believe improvement is needed.

Peer Feedback:

Seek feedback from a colleague, team member, or mentor regarding your leadership approach. Ask for their honest assessment of your strengths and areas that require enhancement. This external perspective can offer valuable insights.

Action Plan:

Based on your self-assessment and peer feedback, create a specific action plan to enhance your leadership in empowering others and cultivating a culture of trust and collaboration. Consider the following questions:

- What concrete steps can I take to assign my team members better?
- How can I actively contribute to a culture of trust and collaboration within my organization?
- What strategies can I implement to nurture new leaders within my team or department?
- Are there resources or training opportunities that can aid in my leadership development?

Implementation:

Commit to implementing your action plan. Start with small, manageable steps and gradually work toward your larger goals. Monitor your progress regularly and be open to adjustments as needed.

Reflect and Iterate:

Periodically revisit your action plan and reflect on your leadership journey. Celebrate your successes and acknowledge areas where further improvement is required. Adjust your project as you continue to grow as a leader.

Remember that leadership is an ongoing process of growth and self-improvement. By actively seeking ways to empower others and create a culture of trust, you can strengthen your leadership capabilities and positively impact your organization.

YOU ARE YOUR MOST IMPORTANT BRAND

"Your smile is your logo, your personality is your business card, how you leave others feeling after an experience with you becomes your trademark."
—Jay Danzie

As you dedicate your time and efforts to building other people's businesses, never forget to cultivate *your* own personal brand. Unlike corporate roles that may be subject to layoffs, shifting bosses, or economic downturns, your brand will follow you throughout your career. No one can take that away from you.

Developing our brand is an ongoing process influenced by our actions and thought leadership. Our connections and contributions strengthen it. However, many people begin networking and building their brands too late—never having time while employed, they wait until they leave their companies and start their job hunt, not realizing that relationship building and thought leadership are a continuous process.

We often invest our time and money in other people's brands, wearing logos like badges of honor. Throughout my journey, I dedicated myself to building other people's brands and companies despite having no actual ownership. When I was laid off a few years back, I realized I had devoted my energy to brands and companies that didn't value me beyond being a line item. Aside from a few stock options, I had no ownership in these brands I had worked tirelessly to build.

Here's a pivotal realization: Your voice matters. Your thoughts matter.

As an introvert, I initially grappled with the idea of self-promotion, deeming it too self-indulgent. It made me uncomfortable. But as I built my business, I realized I needed to develop my brand to achieve all my financial and business goals. I am the product. Or, to quote Jay-Z, "I'm not a businessman...I'm a business, man."

Time is an irreplaceable currency, and making the most of it is paramount. Seize the opportunity to live an extraordinary life—playing small does not lead to exceptional outcomes. Remember this enduring truth: Your brand is the most essential brand you will ever wear. So invest in it, nurture it, and let it flourish throughout your lifetime.

💡 Exercise: Create Your Brand Statement

Take some time to reflect on your values, strengths, and passions. Consider the qualities that make you unique and the kind of impact you want to have on others. Then, write a personal brand statement that captures the essence of who you are and what you want to be known for.

Here's a template to get you started:

"I am [Your Name], and I am known for [list your key qualities, strengths, and values]. My mission is to [describe your mission or the impact you want to make]. Through [your actions or activities], I aim to [describe the positive change or influence you want to create]."

For example:

"I am Jane Smith, known for my creativity, empathy, and dedication to personal growth. My mission is to inspire and empower others to unlock their creative potential and lead fulfilling lives. Through my writing, workshops, and coaching, I aim to help people tap into their inner creativity and find joy in the creative process."

Once you've crafted your brand statement, revisit it regularly and refine it as needed. This statement will serve as a guiding light for building your brand and staying true to your values and goals.

HONOR YOUR WORDS

"You are what you do, not what you say you'll do."
—Carl Jung

Words hold power, but it's through action that our reality is crafted. Are you a person who follows through on their word? Upholding your commitments and promises is the most profound way to cultivate self-trust and self-respect.

Don't merely discuss your aspirations—pursue them with unwavering passion.

Don't merely declare your love for your family—invest time in them and cherish every moment.

Don't just profess love for your children—engage with them and revel in shared experiences.

Don't just announce your intention to attain good health—quit harmful habits like smoking and immerse yourself in refreshing nature walks.

Don't just claim to possess faith—demonstrate it by serving others through meaningful actions.

Words undeniably hold significance, but the transformational power of action is what truly matters.

💡 Exercise: Are You Upholding Your Self-Commitments?

Let's contemplate the numerous commitments we make to ourselves, often left by the wayside. Think of our countless New Year's resolutions, only to abandon them later. Whether it's the aspiration to shed 10 pounds or the promise of regular date nights with your partner, the list of unfulfilled self-promises can be extensive. Each time we stumble on a commitment to ourselves, we chip away at our self-trust.

Instead of crafting grand, often unattainable goals that inevitably crumble, consider focusing on actions you can seamlessly incorporate into your daily life. Rather than vowing to lose 10 pounds, set a practical objective like taking a 5-minute walk after each meal. Redirect your attention toward goals that you can faithfully uphold daily."

KEEP GOING

"Whenever you find yourself doubting how far you can go, just remember how far you have come. Remember everything you have faced, all the battles you have won, and all the fears you have overcome."
—N.R. Walker

Persevere, my friend!
You've come so far.
Press onward.

You've navigated an arduous and winding path, conquering obstacles that once loomed insurmountable. Behind you, a trail of victories is testimony to your unwavering resilience and relentless determination.

Keep going.

In the face of uncertain tomorrows and the weight of past missteps, anchor yourself firmly in the present. Embrace your progress, for it serves as the driving force propelling you ahead. Keep your gaze fixed on the distant horizon, for your journey is far from over. Keep forging ahead!

Often, we focus on past mistakes and future fears. Instead, focus on the here and now. And if you intentionally choose to reflect on the past, channel your attention toward the strides you've made. This is far more valuable than lamenting what might have been.

💡 Exercise: Grab a Sheet of Paper, and Let's Celebrate!

Jot down 20 of your most significant victories—those grand dreams that turned into your reality and the small triumphs that brought you joy. Remember those moments when you defied the odds and emerged even stronger.

As the ink flows, let it stir feelings of accomplishment and resilience within you. You've conquered so much; this list is a testament to your indomitable spirit. Cherish these victories and carry them forward as inspiration for your future endeavors.

YOU ARE A WORK IN PROGRESS

"We are all rough drafts of the people we're becoming."
—Bob Goff

Embrace the idea that your evolution is an ongoing journey. There is no finish line. Much like the intricate process of crafting a fine work of art, grant yourself the freedom to edit and refine as you progress toward becoming the unique masterpiece you are destined to be. Channel your inner Picasso!

Recognize that self-discovery is a boundless expedition with no final destination; it is a continuous odyssey. While traversing various life phases, it's natural for your genuine self to adjust and develop. Embrace these changes as opportunities for personal growth and transformation. Take a moment to appreciate where you stand today and celebrate the strides you've made while striving to become a better version of yourself tomorrow.

💡 Exercise: I Am My Own Masterpiece

Find a quiet and comfortable space where you can focus without distractions. Begin by reflecting on the idea that your personal growth and self-discovery are continuous processes with no fixed endpoint.

Grab a blank sheet of paper and a pen or pencil. Write at the top of the sheet: "My Masterpiece of Self."

Now, think about your life journey and the different phases you've gone through. Consider your achievements, experiences, and personal growth.

Start jotting down key milestones, achievements, and personal qualities that define who you are today. These could be significant life events, individual strengths, values, or positive changes you've made.

Embrace the notion that just like a masterpiece, you have the power to edit and refine your life as you go along. Write down a few aspects of yourself or your life that you want to improve.

Reflect on how you've adapted and evolved in response to various life challenges and experiences. Write down a few instances where you've demonstrated resilience and growth.

Use this exercise as an opportunity to appreciate your journey and the progress you've made so far.

Consider keeping a journal to track your ongoing personal growth and evolution. You can use it to set goals, document changes, and celebrate achievements.

After completing the exercise, take a moment to reflect on your newfound perspective about your ongoing self-evolution. Consider applying this awareness to your daily life and future goals.

Remember that personal growth is a lifelong journey; this exercise can remind you to embrace the process and strive to become your best version.

CHARACTER MATTERS

"Try not to become a man of success. Rather become a man of value."
—Albert Einstein

The measure of your character can be found in how you treat those who can offer you nothing in return. Consider how you interact with the wait-staff or individuals without titles, fame, or influence.

In a world that often glorifies social status, strive to be the person whose kindness extends to every station in life. Your treatment of others serves as a clear reflection of your character.

Which character traits do you hold in high regard when you observe them in others? Are you actively embodying these traits? If not, identify the qualities worth adopting, document them, and pledge to nurture them within yourself.

Exercise: Character Reflection and Growth

Start by making two lists in your notebook:

List 1: "Character Traits I Admire in Others"

> In this list, write down character traits you genuinely admire when observing them in others. These could include kindness, empathy, honesty, humility, generosity, patience, and more. Take your time to think about qualities that resonate with you.

List 2: "Character Traits I Want to Emulate"

> In this list, identify which character traits from List 1 you want to incorporate into your personality actively. Be specific about the characteristics you wish to strengthen within yourself.

Once you've completed both lists, take a moment to reflect on the traits you want to cultivate in yourself.

Write a short paragraph or two for each trait you want to emulate, explaining why it is important and how it can positively impact your interactions with others and your life.

Consider creating a plan for how you can work on developing these traits. This might include setting specific goals or actions to practice in your daily life.

Commit to this journey of character development. Write a personal commitment statement expressing your dedication to nurturing these traits within yourself.

Keep your notebook or paper where you can revisit it regularly for inspiration and to track your progress.

Remember that personal character growth is an ongoing process, and this exercise serves as a starting point for self-improvement. Over time, you can reflect on your journey and make adjustments to continue strengthening the traits that matter most to you.

Someday you will look back
on all the progress you made
and be so glad that you
didn't give up. Keep going.
You got this.
I am so proud of you. Thank
you for not giving up on us.

I Love You,
Your Future Self

DON'T GIVE UP. YOUR FUTURE SELF WILL THANK YOU

Recall a time when you embarked on a new exercise program, launched a business, or undertook a new project. It's always fun in the beginning. We get swept away with the excitement of building something new.

But then things inevitably get tough.
We encounter setbacks.
Things get complicated as multiple commitments arise.

It gets messy in the middle.
We lose motivation.
Monotony and tedium set in.

Here's the thing: if you want to get better, you can't quit when things get tough. If it truly matters to you, it's essential you see it through. To get better at anything, you must do hard things, daily. Things aren't always going to be easy.

While we live in a world that focuses on the big milestones and achievements, our success usually comes down to doing hard things daily. Yes, the mundane grunt work.
If you want success, it's about maintaining consistency.
It's about showing up, even when you don't want to get out of bed.

It's having faith in yourself when self-doubt creeps in.
It's about taking action even when it scares the shit out of you. It's showing up. It's about starting when you're not ready.

Just keep going. Your future self will be so proud of you!

YOU ARE BECOMING

"What you become in the process is more important than the dream."
—Les Brown

Never underestimate how vital the small victories were towards your journey of self-discovery. They compounded and created the person you are today. Ultimately, the person we become takes greater significance than the ultimate triumph we achieve.

Pause and celebrate:

- The obstacles you've conquered.
- The sacrifices you've willingly made.
- Your relentless determination during the most challenging moments.
- The invaluable support you've received from others.
- Your personal growth and the remarkable individual you're evolving into.

In a world that often fixates on the importance of winning, take a moment to pay homage to the transformative process. Achieving your desires may be a fleeting moment, but the evolution into the person you are destined to become is an enduring and profound journey.

💡 Exercise: Reflect on Your Progress

Whether you embarked on this book's journey yesterday or a year ago, take a moment to contemplate the strides you've made since then. What accomplishments along the path of self-discovery fill you with the greatest sense of pride?

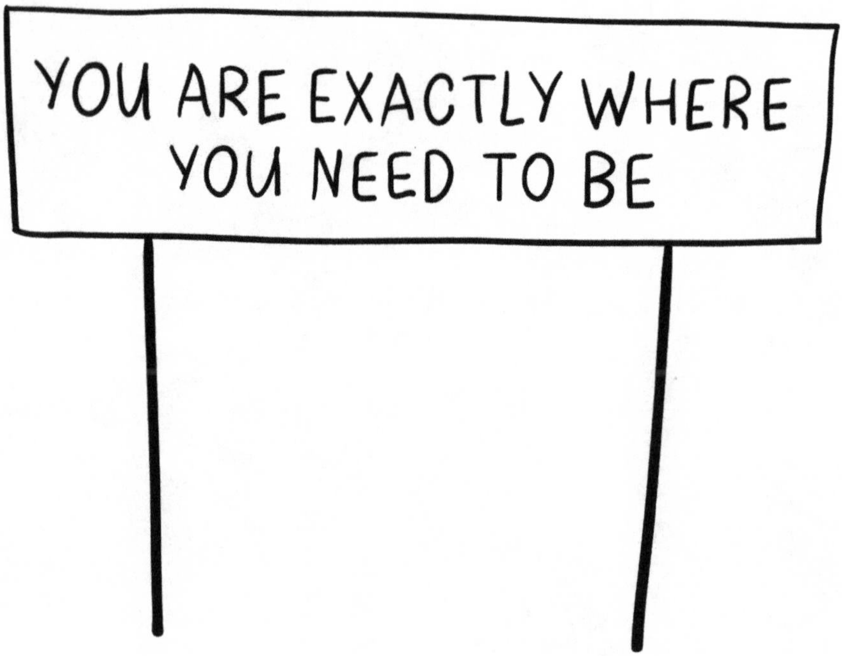
YOU ARE EXACTLY WHERE
YOU NEED TO BE

"If you were waiting for a sign, this is it.

You Are Exactly Where You Need To Be

Keep going. That's it. That's the message."

–Lan Phan

CONCLUSION

Create a Life Worth Living.

The average person is granted 27,375 days of life. My earnest wish for you is to infuse purpose into each one of those days.

As I find myself halfway through my life's journey, I reflect on how much of it was spent—almost 40 percent—unduly concerned about others' opinions, pursuing paths dictated by external forces, and relentlessly chasing titles and promotions while neglecting my aspirations and what I loved most. It's this realization that fueled my desire to pen this book.

Living a life with intentionality is no easy feat; it requires grit and resilience. Yet I can attest that when you deliberately craft your life, you inch closer to becoming the person you've always aspired to be. You draw nearer to a life brimming with fulfillment, purpose, and joy.

You edge closer to discovering your Ikigai, your reason for being.

In many so-called "self-help" books (a term I dislike and the industry, in general), the message often revolves around amassing wealth, fame, and material desires. In this book, I hope to convey a different narrative—one of releasing the expectations and stories that have been forced upon you.

Here's the spoiler alert. There are no secrets in this book. You already know all of this. This book is just here to remind you.

Instead, I encourage you to blaze your own trail, grounded in the wisdom of four fundamental lessons:

Lesson 1: Determine what holds the utmost significance in your life.
Lesson 2: Cultivate a mindset that aligns with your life's purpose.
Lesson 3: Take the initial steps toward manifesting your purpose.
Lesson 4: Commit to living out your purpose daily and aiding others in doing the same.

These lessons may not introduce you to groundbreaking revelations; instead, they serve as gentle reminders of what you already know deep within. I believe that we all know the answer to our story, we just need to listen to that quiet voice within it moving us towards the directions of our authentic life.

Love,

ACKNOWLEDGEMENTS

I want to extend my heartfelt gratitude to my family who have played a pivotal role in my life and in the creation of this book.

First and foremost, my gratitude goes to my loving husband, Kevin Messam, whose unwavering support and encouragement have been my constant source of inspiration. To my precious daughter, Morgan, your presence brings boundless joy to my life, and I hope this book serves as a testament to what can be achieved with dedication and passion.

I want to remember my mother, Mai, who has been a guiding light throughout my life. You have sacrificed so much for us, and I will never forget the lessons you have taught me. And to my father, who is no longer with us, I hope that my efforts have made you proud and that your spirit continues to inspire me.

I'm also thankful for the enduring support of my brothers, Van, and Khanh Phan, whose support and encouragement have been invaluable on this journey. Special shoutout to Van, you helped guide me when we lost dad and you've remained a guiding force in my life. Even today, you and Huan (my bonus brother) are two of the most generous people I know.

And to my extended family in-laws, to Marlene who took 6-months off to help us with new born Morgan when I never changed a diaper in my life. To Delroy who is the best papa in the world. Darren, Jhanelle, Ava, Renette, David, thank you for welcoming me into your family and always making feel at home.

Lastly, I want to acknowledge my dear friend and sister from another mother, Mita Mallick. Your friendship has enriched my life in countless ways, and your unwavering support means the world to me. This book would not have happened without your encouragement and belief in me. Sometimes when we lose our light we need to borrow from our friends. You are that light to me.

To each of my friends who I hold in my heart, you know who you are, I want to emphasize that I am who I am today because of your love, support, and belief in me. This book reflects our shared experiences, and I am deeply grateful for the role each of you has played in shaping both my life and this work.

ABOUT THE AUTHOR

Lan Phan is an author and speaker known for her expertise in purpose, mindset, and continuous improvement. Her expertise has made her a sought-after consultant for Fortune 500 companies, where she advises CEOs, and C-Suite executives to help them navigate the dynamic realms of business and innovation. Her thought leadership can be found in prestigious publications like The Harvard Business Review, Forbes, and Money.

As a keynote speaker, Lan has graced prominent platforms including the United Nations, Stanford University, NYU Law, and events hosted by Fortune 100 companies like PepsiCo, Warner Media, Citi, Bank of America, Disney, Meta. On LinkedIn and YouTube her content reaches an audience of millions annually, resonating deeply across diverse demographics.

A Stanford University alumnus, she was honored with the J.E. Wallace Sterling Award, recognizing her significant impact through leadership and community service. She also holds master's degree from the Harvard Graduate School of Education. Lan resides in New York with her husband, Kevin and their daughter Morgan.

Contact Lan for interviews, speaking, or training opportunities.

Email: info@communityofseven.com
Website: www.LanPhan.co
www.communityofseven.com
linkedin.com/in/lanphan

CONNECT WITH LAN

Lan is on a mission to help leaders and companies find their purpose and reason for being. She helps people discover their 'why' and find success in their businesses. Ways you can work with Lan include speaking and moderating opportunities, programming, culture and community strategy consultation, leadership training & development and consulting. She helps leaders go from knowledge to action.

She is available for public speaking, seminars, and workshops.

Connect with Lan:

- Website: www.lanphan.co
- Email: info@communityofseven.com

For additional free content and workbook go to www.lanphan.co